OUTDOORS
in new zealand

colin moore

JK,   December 2003

Hope this book inspires

you to come visit soon!

Merry Christmas!

xo Robyn, Cris

3

Cheeky

NH
NEW
HOLLAND

For my children, Rupert and Naivasha, and my friend Joe, who have been my happy companions on many adventures and always given encouragement, and my wife, Fran, who is there waiting patiently when we return.

First published in 2002 by New Holland Publishers (NZ) Ltd
Auckland • Sydney • London • Cape Town

218 Lake Road, Northcote, Auckland, New Zealand
14 Aquatic Drive, Frenchs Forest, NSW 2086, Australia
86 Edgware Road, London W2 2EA, United Kingdom
80 McKenzie Street, Cape Town 8001, South Africa

www.newhollandpublishers.com

ISBN: 1 877246 91 3

Publishing manager: Renée Lang
Design and typesetting: Alison Dench
Editor: Alison Dench
Front cover photograph: Geoff Dale

Printed by Times Offset (M) Sdn Bhd, Malaysia

contents

acknowledgements

My modest adventures in the outdoors owe much to the experience of my companions and I am fortunate to have enjoyed the guidance of some of the best. Several are mentioned in the text. Special mentors have been Joe Scott-Woods of the Alpine Sports Club, Peter Sommerhalder of the Auckland Canoe Centre, Neil Hunt of the Snowcentre and Scott Lee for invaluable help with skiing, the late Gary Ball for introducing me to basic snow and ice skills, John Giacon of New Zealand Angling for fly fishing guidance, Chris Smith for sailing a classic yacht, Chris Bradbeer for his company on many adventures, and other outdoors people too numerous to mention.

The 'Outdoors' column from which this book springs would have died without the support of *New Zealand Herald* editors Peter Scherer and Gavin Ellis, and the encouragement of many colleagues, particularly Bruce Morris and Peter Jessup. I have been sustained over the years by numerous readers who have gone out of their way to pass compliments, and I thank them, particularly my greatest fans, my mother and my late father. I am grateful to the *New Zealand Herald* for waiving any copyright claims.

I would like to thank Alison Dench, who brought her own enthusiasm for the outdoors to her work editing and designing this book. Most of all, perhaps, I should thank Renée Lang of New Holland Publishers, who has proved the existence of serendipity and that when one door closes another may indeed open.

introduction

Like most New Zealanders, I grew up with the outdoors at the back door. Ours was a world of open spaces, trees to climb and build huts in, places to camp, and streams and estuaries to catch small fish and mess about in boats on. The background for our make-believe play adventures, even in an urban environment, was just a smaller version of our wonderfully varied landscape.

Apart from a few modest adventures and a succession of small sailboats, I didn't follow this nurturing in the outdoors into tramping, climbing and the like – other activities intruded, such as competitive sport and music, but the legacy was often apparent during OE travels and when working in Europe. Whatever our recreational bent, we are by upbringing, familiarity and instinct a people comfortable with the outdoors, and unlikely to be fazed when we step, or are forced, outside our comfort zones. More important, perhaps, than any latent settler skills is a general passion for the natural environment. New Zealanders may have been somewhat dubious guardians of island Aotearoa but most of us have a genuine concern and appreciation for the environment. We are instinctive conservationists and likely to be more in awe of the cathedrals of nature than we are those of humankind.

Those instincts saw me flirt with becoming a professional forester, a notion soon dulled by peering down microscopes at plant cells and dissecting rotting fish. A vocational guidance advisor, perhaps influenced by my results in English, suggested I might make a journalist and the *New Zealand Herald* gave me a job as a cadet reporter. It was a move, mostly indoors, that I have never regretted and, ironically, that has given me greater opportunities to enjoy the New Zealand outdoors than I probably would have had as a forester.

My proper introduction to the outdoors came relatively late in life, when I took up skiing. This led to other mountain activities, and the major impetus came with my becoming a father. The best way to get more adventures in the mountains was to write about them, which I did frequently. In 1987 I persuaded the *Herald* features editor that outdoor recreation deserved a regular column. It was the centenary year of New Zealand's national parks and an appropriate time to acknowledge the huge and ongoing popularity of outdoor pursuits.

My first 'Outdoors' column in the *New Zealand Herald* was published on 28 February 1987. There were only two criteria: the activities must be outdoors and non-competitive, so the column has featured everything from flying kites to climbing Mt Cook. At first it was a reporting job; I mainly wrote about other people's activities. But my children took me into outdoor adventures of our own – you can't carry youngsters on your back into a nightclub or concert hall – and when I wrote about our modest journeys I found readers enjoyed the stories.

One of the compliments I am most proud of came from the noted knee-injury specialist and surgeon, Barry Tietjens. He said that he enjoyed my columns because they were 'non-threatening' and that his wife would sometimes put a clipping under the fridge magnet and ask why their family didn't do 'something like this'. That was exactly what I hoped my stories would do: inspire readers into some adventures of their own.

Over the years I have become more confident in writing about my own fairly modest activities but I pretend to be nothing other than a journalist. I am, as a colleague on London's *Daily Telegraph* once remarked, 'a man on the sidewalk of life with a notebook and pencil in hand'. The sidewalk I love most is the New Zealand outdoors. It is this country's greatest resource and it was why I happily bid Fleet Street goodbye.

This is not a guide book or a how-to book. I am an advocate, not an expert witness. It is a collection of 'Outdoors' columns spanning several years, chosen to be representative of the variety of outdoor adventures easily available and achievable, and because, I hope, they are a 'good read'. The stories are intended to encourage people to embark on adventures of their own, not necessarily those described. Where necessary the text has been updated and edited and an information panel included. The reference sources given are from my personal library and some books may now be out of print. However, they should be available in public libraries.

When newspaper or magazine clippings lie under a fridge magnet it is a revealing test of whether the stories have made an impression on a reader. This collection of columns may be too bulky to be given the fridge treatment. But I will be happily satisfied if it inspires you to step outside and enjoy the wonder of the New Zealand outdoors.

Mangonui
State Forest

WHANGAREI

Northern
Coromandel

Long Bay-Okura

Waitakere
Ranges &
West Coast

AUCKLAND

THAMES

Kaimai Range

TAURANGA

HAMILTON

ROTORUA

Raukumara
Range

TAUPO

GISBORNE

NEW PLYMOUTH

TURANGI

NAPIER/
HASTINGS

WANGANUI

PALMERSTON
NORTH

WELLINGTON

bushed!

Fire and axe stripped New Zealand
of much of its native forest cover but
what remains is the quintessential Kiwi
outdoors, the bush. You never tire of
walking in it, even when you're bushed.

on the trail of true enjoyment

My first editor at the *Herald*, O.S. Hintz, was a large and lugubrious man whose only communication with lowly cadets was something between a grunt and growl. Hintz was at least passionate about trout fishing, and years after I had heard his last growl I found his book on Taupo trout fishing in a second-hand bookstore in Queenstown. I bought it to read in front of the open fire in the bar of Eichardt's Hotel while the rain beat outside and the Coronet Peak ski field stayed firmly closed. And there I read: 'A good half of true enjoyment is the pursuit of pleasure that can be happily shared.'

Perhaps because I was on my own or perhaps because of my surprise that the sentiment was from Hintz, I marked the passage and have written it on the front page of my diary ever since.

Hintz was a trout fisher, not a tramper, but his observation on true enjoyment was never more appropriate than on a mid-week ramble in the Goldie Bush and Motutara Scenic Reserves in the Waitakere Ranges. A quartet of the retired, semi-retired, self-employed and self-indulgent, we have the good fortune to be able to sneak away while others are hard at their labours. We might have had golf clubs in the boot of the car or trout-fishing rods, but on this day our pursuit to be shared requires tramping boots, a walking staff, water bottle and packed lunch.

I have passed the entrance to Goldie Bush in Constable Road, near Muriwai, several times, because the Te Henga Walkway – that wonderful trail along the rugged west coast to Bethells Beach and a link between the parkland of the Waitakeres and Muriwai Regional Park – also begins in Constable Road. But I have never previously stopped to investigate the reserve, which is a sort of outlier of regenerating native bush to the north of the bulk of the bush-clad Waitakeres. Its recent history lies in logging and while that may, for a few generations anyway, mean that its kauri stands are a long way short of deserving the title magnificent, it does give the reserves an additional dimension. The logging tracks and skids are easily discernible. So is the base of an old kauri dam in the Mokoroa Stream, whose pent-up waters would once have sent logs rushing down-stream.

There is a loop track through the two reserves totalling about 6.4km and taking a comfortable 3½ hours to complete. You can join at Constable Road, as we do, or at the other end of the loop at Horseman Road. Or,

if you organise shuttle transport, you can go just one way.

From Constable Road the trail winds downhill until it reaches the Mokoroa Stream. I love stream bashing. It is quintessential New Zealand tramping – wading up and across streams in strong and well-oiled leather boots, the water intoxicating your senses with its many colours and its tonal range. Ferns and flax overhang the banks and often as not a fantail, hoping your passage will disturb some tasty insects, will follow you, darting ahead and then slipping behind.

The stream route runs more alongside the Mokoroa Stream than through it, but while traversing it is not strictly a stream bash, you do have to make sufficient crossings to get that feeling of an adventure into the unknown. Now and again the stream-bed has been dropped by the forces of nature into large steps that the water cascades down and that you must cross over – with care if you don't want to slip to an unwelcome swim. In summer it would take very little persuasion to cool off in the waterholes.

About 2.5km along the stream is our goal, the Mokoroa Falls. They are framed by bush and tumble into a large pool. It's a delightful spot and would be superb for a summer picnic, but this is winter and the stream is in shade, so we climb to a lookout opposite the falls where the sun warms a large rock on which we stop for lunch.

I don't think we oldies in Goldie have stopped talking since we set off. We are catching up on a lot of gossip and news of recent adventures and this sunny, midwinter day in the tranquillity of the Waitakere Ranges bush has us drunk with the satisfaction of our good fortune to be in this spot. We babble along like the stream below us.

Our route back to Constable Road is along a ridge through regenerating kauri and kanuka. Some stands of kauri rickers are as thickly packed as a maize field. Not all will survive the coming centuries to become forest giants, but there is no shortage of candidates from which nature can choose the fittest.

It is reassuring. Our happy quartet won't be around to see the forest return to its former glory, but we have seen its promise and shared the magic, albeit briefly, of the New Zealand bush. It is, as Hintz so rightly wrote, true enjoyment, happily shared.

a wade in the ranges

It seems ironic that Mt Hikurangi in the Raukumara Range should be the first place on mainland New Zealand to catch the sun each day. Ironic because the range, which rises steeply from two coastlines to create the huge bulge of the North Island, also catches an extraordinary amount of rain.

But then the Raukumara is paradox. It is one of the few mountain areas in New Zealand that is wetter east of the main range, with the mountains sucking the moisture from southerly and easterly winds. It straddles the same latitude as Melbourne and on its highest tops there is snow and alpine flora. At lower altitudes the thick and mostly unmodified bush is a confusing collection of species usually not found together. And nurturing them is a mix of ancient and quite recent sedimentary soils distorted by volcanism and the buckling of the Hikurangi Trench. The rain, the high humidity and the freezing tops often shatter land that erodes down the steepest ridges. When storms such as Cyclone Bola hit, they leave a tangle of windfall and impenetrable undergrowth.

The Maori ventured into this bird-rich wilderness to collect food or to lick the wounds of battle in the secret reaches of some of its fearsomely steep gorges. And by ancient trail the East Coast tribes would travel from coast to coast across the remote interior.

In December 1842 Bishop Selwyn took a short-cut from Rangitukia to Opotiki on a 'war path' across the Raukumara. Trampers and hunters, who consider the paradoxical range one of the toughest tests of bushcraft and navigational skills, call the trail from Tapuaeroa River to Te Kaha the Selwyn route.

It is a place where most need the safety of numbers, so the chance to go there comes infrequently The bishop's diary noted that he had '20 natives laden with food and armed with hatchets'. On a long weekend we have 22 trampers from the Auckland and Catholic Tramping Clubs laden with 'de-hy' food and armed with polyprop clothing and parkas for a trip that has even tempted one member to book from Canada.

That sort of enthusiasm deserves better weather but the Raukumara has other ideas. It brings the bus to a wheel-slipping halt a couple of kilometres early on a muddy trail and challenges the group to go for it. The rain is almost a refreshing relief after the close-quarters of an all-night bus trip. If there is any problem it is only because it is a steep ridge climb out of the Tapuaeroa River catchment over the 1005m summit of Te Ranganuiatoi. And in this humidity it is as damp inside my parka as it is out.

Bush lore suggests you go up ridges and down streams and that is the way our leader John Tasker takes us. There is a faint trail that runs out as we breach the summit and begin our descent to the Okapua Stream. Tasker has been here before but it is still map-and-compass tramping. This land is so deeply dissected by the forces of nature that just a few metres of poor navigation can lead to the wrong stream-bed.

We sidle along a scree trail and down into the ribbon of the stream's headwaters. The bush almost covers the boulder-strewn path the water is taking but that slippery trail is mostly the only option: except in a few places, the sides of the stream are too steep or overgrown to contemplate tramping through, particularly when there is a stream-bed to follow.

On the bus down Tasker had passed around a copy of the bishop's diary entry. It was too difficult to read in the jolting bus, which is perhaps as well because on 7 December 1842, Selwyn recorded: 'Travellers more minutely curious than myself would have counted the exact number of fordings; but I contented myself with the general impression that it is a day of as much wading as walking.'

Thus, like Selwyn, we begin to wade our way across the Raukumara Range. It is difficult going because the rocks are treacherously slippery with slime that has built up since the last flood. Worst of all are logs that have long ago fallen into the stream to become obstacles as feared and dangerous as black ice. We quickly learn to avoid them. Hand-holds on the log-jam debris can be just as precarious. Grasping something for support may be your undoing.

There are two groups in the party – an explorers' group under Tasker and a medium group under another leader. After day one they will take different routes. By mid-afternoon we are strung out along the rising stream. It is getting dark when we reach a shingle bank but I am advised against camping on the beach. I drape a flysheet over a log on the bank and make a meal as best I can, in torchlight, before crawling into a bivvy bag and settling down for the night.

The next morning when I look over the log the beach below has become a fast-moving torrent of grey water. Tasker has us up at 6.30am and we are away an hour later. It is less than half an hour's walk to the Raukokore River. This is one of those fabled waterways of immense tradition and eerie magic. It catches the headwaters of the Raukumara Range and is a tribal boundary between Ngati Porou on the east of the range and Whanau-a-Apanui on the west.

Near the confluence with the Okapua Stream is the hunters' camp where we had intended to camp the previous night. In fine weather and summer daylight it must be a wonderful place to while away some hours. The Selwyn route is down-river to the Tangitarua Stream, which it follows up to a steep bush saddle before moving down the Arawhata Stream to the Kereu River. But Tasker has already done that journey, so the explorers' party heads up-river until we reach a stream unnamed on topographical maps.

The Raukokore has been a pleasant but all too brief respite from stream bashing. We return to boulder-hopping and log-jam negotiating. It seems easier than the day before but perhaps I am getting used to it. We are travelling north-east, climbing higher and higher. Small streams join the one we are in and Tasker constantly checks his compass and map.

Selwyn wrote of clambering up a stream-bed 'till it parted in three branches, where we came to stand, our guides being in doubt. At last one of the party discovered a fragment of a firebrand which decided the point.' We make no such helping discovery but eventually, when the stream becomes a drain, we clamber out and climb through a jungle of supplejack up a steep spur.

As we gain height we realise that we probably should have taken another stream branch but Tasker gets his bearings and we traverse the spur and stop for lunch just above the saddle we are looking for. There is no mistaking the saddle. The land rises steeply in two directions and drops steeply in the other two.

We move downhill into another unnamed stream. Soon our stream bashing begins again but now we know we are on the other side of the range. The deep pools and high walls of this watercourse are beautiful, but I am near the end of my tether when Tasker comes back upstream to tell me our campsite on the Kereu River is just a few minutes downstream.There is still another day to go before we get to Mangaroa Station and Te Kaha but I feel slightly euphoric. The challenge is all but completed. Even the rain cannot dampen the achievement.

But it is not quite over because next morning, before the Kereu opens out to wide shingle banks, we must first negotiate a couple of kilometres of spectacular gorge. It involves considerable rock-hopping and log-jam jumping. I watch the nimble, casually balanced Tasker. Where he takes three evenly spaced strides to negotiate one hazardous stretch, I take eight clumsy, drunken paces. A week later my knees and ankles still feel the effects – I doubt our leader has even a twinge. But the satisfaction at crossing the range is surely mutual.

There is possibly no better place from which to start a three-day tramp in the North Island than from the hot mineral pools at Te Aroha Domain. Here you can leave a vehicle with confidence that the friendly folk who run the mineral spa complex and the man in the adjoining kiosk will do their best to ensure it is still waiting and in one piece on your return. The chance to soak in a hot pool will be waiting, too.

But there may be no more sobering a way to begin an outdoor adventure and quickly sort out the fit from the dreamers than to head into the bush up and over the 953m bulk of Mt Te Aroha. As a day walk, the climb to the highest point in the Kaimai Range is one of the best there is close to Auckland, with magnificent views of the Hauraki Plains as far west as Mt Taranaki, and down the spine of the range to East Cape. As a gateway into the interior, for limbs that have not had a lot of recent use and with a rucksack still heavy with food, it proves a punishing choice.

Yet it is the logical beginning for a modest foray into the Kaimai Range that will take us on a circuit over the range to Katikati Forest and north along Waitawheta valley before recrossing the range and traversing back to Te Aroha and those hot pools. The trail to the top of the 349m Bald Spur is easy going but there is steeper ahead and lazy lungs start pounding as we head towards the summit mist.

It is drizzling when we reach the shelter of the television tower complex on the summit but a quick family debate rules that we press on. Our goal is the 16-bunk Waitawheta Hut, on the eastern side of the range, which should be about 6 hours' walk from our car. But it was after lunch when we began and as we crest the range it is still several hours to the hut, the light is already growing dim and the weather is as damp as our spirits.

This could be the beginning of one of the mini-epics my children complain I am renowned for, but Fate is kind this time. Out of the mist looms a small hut that managed to survive post-Cave Creek paranoia and the DOC penchant for removing anything its budget won't allow it to keep in pristine condition. The three-bunk hut is not marked on maps but it saves us from an unhappy tramp in the dark and wet. Instead we roll out our bedrolls, cook up a hot meal and light a small fire in the hearth to revive our spirits and dry wet clothes.

There is a DOC hut book in this nameless refuge and before we leave under leaden skies in the morning we enter a plea that others who may be caught out by rain and a late start sometime in the future will find a haven too. Just how lucky we were to find the small hut becomes apparent as we stumble downhill through podocarp-hardwood forest of stunted silver beech that grows no further north, tanekaha and miro, to the Waitawheta Hut. The track has become a natural watercourse gouged out by rain and in places reduced to a slippery bare clay ditch that would have been no fun to navigate by torchlight. The hut, though, sits in a delightful location in a remnant kauri forest beside the Waipapa Stream.

The trail follows the Waitawheta River along an old bush tramline once used for kauri logging and it is as good as river valley tramping gets despite the wet. In fact, the rain only adds to the experience. It has not been heavy enough to make the several river crossings involved – the tramline trestle bridges have long since gone – at all dodgy. But the dripping foliage and steaming undergrowth heighten the primeval experience of being embraced by what on this occasion can safely be called a rain forest.

Rivers and streams – and the Waitawheta at this point is not much more than a wide, shallow stream – have a distinct allure under these conditions. The water takes on the colour of weak tea as it picks up tannin from rotting vegetation yet it still reveals the stones and gravel it bubbles over. There is another attraction in this valley trail. It owes its origins to ancient volcanic activity and the geology that once attracted mineral prospectors has in places on the river bank left stunning rock outcrops that aeons of water flow have not managed to erode.

Our route leaves the river to return west to the Dalys Clearing Hut, a spacious 18-bunk hut near the Romanga Stream. We have it to ourselves, although there has been a recent visitor. A note asks any who might come by to keep a lookout for a lost black-and-tan pig dog. There are signs that deer sometimes visit too, to feed on the grass in the clearing.

There is a break in the weather next day for our traverse to Te Aroha along the upper flank of the range. Now birds and cicadas loudly rejoice in the warmth and drying bush. When we stop for a break we are joined by a man and a pack of well-behaved dogs. He is the note writer and he is still searching, as he has been for several days, for his beloved dog.

He carries only a small daypack and his route just that morning would have taken us several days. He tells us that when hunting he carries only dry snack bars that sustain him for days at a time. His dogs all have large collars with a transmitter attached. He carries some metal rods that look like a small television aerial. When the dogs get on to a pig he follows them through the bush to his prey. Well, most times.

We wish him well as we trek on towards Te Aroha. Near the mountain the track descends through the site of the old Tui mine, which worked for lead, zinc and copper between 1967 and 1973 and is still gushing filthy water from its tailings and the rusted remains of its machinery. The mine legacy is a grossly discoloured Tunakohoia Stream.

From there it is a pleasant bush and semi-urban trail back to the domain, the hot pools and our car. The huff and puff three days before now seems worth the effort.

adventure log

GETTING THERE: SH 2 and SH 26 to Te Aroha. The track to the summit of Mt Te Aroha begins in the Te Aroha Domain.

WALKING TIME: One day or several if you intend to cross the Kaimai Range and explore the Waitawheta valley and other areas of the forest park. Tramping from easy to average difficulty close to Auckland and Tauranga.

MAP: LINZ T13

FURTHER INFORMATION: The Kaimai-Mamuku Forest Park PARKMAP gives trail and hut details. See also TRAMPING IN NORTH ISLAND FOREST PARKS by Euan and Jennie Nicol, and WAIKATO WALKS by Graeme Foster. DOC Te Aroha field centre 0-7-884 9303.

around the tip of the peninsula

Here is a riddle. On a clear day you can see Rangitoto and the Sky Tower but it takes about 4 hours to get there. Where is the walk? Okay, here is a clue. Some people might get carsick on the way but the views are stunning, particularly with a setting sun.

Give up? The tip of the Coromandel Peninsula is about as far away as you can get from Auckland without really leaving the region. There are dozens of vantage points in Auckland from where the eastern bulwark of the Hauraki Gulf seems almost close enough to touch. Getting within reach takes a bit more effort, particularly when your destination is Fletcher Bay, where the Pacific Ocean laps at the peninsula's tip.

Yet what the long and winding road from Thames does to some people's stomachs, it more than makes up for with its constant delight of coastal scenery. It is surely the most sustained coastal route in the country and, even without December's blaze of pohutukawa blossoms, is rich in colour.

When the seal stops past Colville, the road seems to hug the foreshore even more closely. Not long ago the public couldn't drive as far as Fletcher Bay. But in the early 1970s the Government bought the peninsula tip and created the Cape Colville Farm Park. It was an inspired decision because, although about a third of the peninsula is managed by DOC, most of those 74,000ha are in the regenerating bush of the ranges.

A coastal park, even though it is mostly in the denuded state in which the European pioneers left it, is a welcome addition to the conservation estate. It is also a welcome adjunct to the recreational riches of the Coromandel Peninsula – to bush-bound tramping, sea kayaking, trout fishing, river running and lots more can be added a coastal trek and mountain-bike ride.

The trek is the Coromandel Walkway from Fletcher Bay to Stony Bay, the road-end on the eastern side of the peninsula. The 7km walkway between the two historic bays is designated under the New Zealand Walkways Act and is a perfect example of the sort of trek that inspired the 1975 legislation. The walkways were intended to be less intimidating than most bush tramps and to encourage people, particularly families, into the outdoors. That very notion brings our two families to Fletcher Bay. The promise is that the 'coastal' walk will not be difficult.

The route between the two bays dates back to the early days of European settlement and is mostly typical of pioneering benched tracks. There are actually two. The coastal track, known as the Six Foot Track, is an old bridle path hewn with pick, shovel and wheelbarrow to link Fletcher Bay and Stony Bay. Further inland is a more direct route cut to drive stock and wide enough to take a four-wheel-drive farm vehicle. It is now an official mountain-bike trail.

DOC's Fletcher Bay campground is one of those delightfully old-fashioned facilities that too often fall prey to progress. It has vault toilets kept meticulously clean three times a day by the people who manage the bay's backpacker hostel, a former farm cottage. A changing room has a cold shower and a good water supply. Some friendly sheep keep the grass down and campers are expected to take their rubbish home. The camp fee of $12 a family is paid into an honesty box.

As beaches go there are nicer examples than Fletcher Bay's stretch of shingle, but the sea rarely comes much clearer or the location more peaceful. Nor does camping come more simple and there are several parties who have made Fletcher Bay their holiday destination and brought their own luxuries. One party has encamped in a derelict concrete blockhouse that was built on the beach to store one bargeload of wool bales. Inside they have a table and chairs, several gas cookers, a kitchen bench, wire shelves full of food and a gas-fired fridge. They have collared this 'possie' before, and the fishing and dive gear around suggests they have good reason.

But we are here to walk so we shoulder packs that have a few too many luxuries in them and set off towards the Six Foot Track. Its description as a coastal walk is a bit misleading because it is over undulating farmland. The view across to Great Barrier and Little Barrier is worth the sweat that a muggy February day soon causes. A brick chimney standing forlornly in a paddock is a monument to the days when all goods came in and out by sailing scow.

Further on is a derelict shepherd's and scrub-cutter's cottage. Walkers have scrawled their passing on its inside walls. The view from the cottage long-drop, straight out to Cuvier Island, ranks as one of the best of that traditional source of scenic inspiration.

There are other monuments to humankind too. Terracing on the knoll that is the northernmost point of the Coromandel Peninsula indicates the site of a former fortified pa. The spot was also once used as a whaling look-out and a coast-watching station during both world wars. On the coast below is a collection of rock pinnacles.

The track drops steeply through bush to Poley Bay. This rocky little cove is not recommended for swimming but in February's heat we take our chances and relish the opportunity to cool off.

'Look, dolphins!' shouts my daughter. And half a dozen dolphins strut their stuff within metres of the shore, sometimes leaping clear of the water.

After the climb out of Poley Bay the track stays on much the same contour but winds in and out of what seems an endless succession of narrow gullies running down to the sea. Stony Bay stays tantalisingly in the distance but fortunately the track tends to be shaded by coastal forest. Beneath us is Shag Bay, and one wit suggests the next is Extremely Buggered Bay.

Stony Bay is exactly that, but its ambience is anything but hard. There are rustic pohutukawa, a freshwater lagoon, grassy camping spots and bush-clad Moehau Mountain, the 891m lord of the range, standing sentinel in the background. The ranger who comes to collect our camp fees says there are sometimes more than 200 people camped at the bay. He is kept busy laying bait stations for possums but defends the voracious marsupials against the charge that they are the cause of the dead pohutukawa we have noticed. That is mainly old age, he says.

For $30 he will ferry walkers back to Fletcher Bay. Our party resists the temptation but splits into two the next day, with one group retracing its steps and the other heading inland. The direct route climbs to 575m but at least the footing is sure. We meet a mountain-biker coming down all smiles – and on the other side meet one struggling uphill, pushing his bike before him.

The coastal route party beat us into Fletcher Bay by about half an hour. The race to the cooling sea is pretty much a tie.

midwinter madness

It is about 24km as the crow flies from Muriwai to Whatipu. To take a crow flight could be handy, because when a chain of volcanic islands exploded out of the sea on what is now Auckland's west coast about 16 million years ago the geological forces did not have road building in mind.

The volcanic rock embedded in ancient silt is a lot tougher than the sandstone of the Auckland isthmus. But so are the westerlies that sweep off the Tasman Sea to blast the 400m-high western barrier of the Waitakere Ranges. Over the aeons streams have eroded the volcanic plateau to cut deep valleys and gorges and expose the lava and volcanic conglomerate. What is left is 10,000ha of rugged bush-clad parkland – and another 7000ha of water catchment reserve – to make a tramper's spectacular backdrop to the city.

Out on the coast to which the streams and deep-sided ridges extend, molten lava that welled up through fractures during further eruptions cooled into blocks that are easily dislodged by pounding surf. The forces sculptured raw cliffs, rock stacks, caves and blowholes, offshore islands and – more recently – sandy bays and broad, constantly changing beaches.

If you are not a crow it is anything between 30km and 36km up and down this dramatic roller-coaster of a coastline. That makes it an ideal 'midwinter madness' tramp for the Alpine Sports and Auckland Catholic Tramping Clubs. It does take a degree of madness to hold one of the longest day tramps on one of the year's shortest days. But this is why a bunch of mad midwinter trekkers are at the start of Te Henga Walkway just as the sun begins to rise over the ranges.

Muriwai Beach is actually about 4km down the road from the northern entrance to this 8km coastal walkway, which is part of the New Zealand national walkway system. The track, starting across farmland before it reaches the coastal heights, is one of the more spectacular in the region because of the rugged power of the west coast, which is almost always just beneath your boots.

It is not a difficult walk and it seems to get shorter each time I make the trek. For some reason it always seems to be sheltered and clothing brought to counter coastal wind is soon consigned to rucksacks. The track has had some care and attention from Friends of Walking, a group of volunteers sponsored by Hannahs and DOC. Some of the muddier or most eroded sections of the track have been bridged and steps have been repaired. The only disappointment on this splendid trail is the mournful sight of the bleached remains of mature pohutukawa trees, killed by possums and unlikely to regenerate.

Just past Raetahinga Point, on the high ground above O'Neill Bay, is one of the west coast's most breathtaking views. Ahead are Erangi Point, Ihumoana Island and the sweep of Te Henga/Bethells Beach. Beyond are four major ridges yet to cross and in the far, far distance the surf breaks across the Manukau Bar to mark journey's end at Whatipu. We stop for a scroggin break on the low saddle between O'Neill Bay and Bethells as the 'fast party' strides down the beach ahead of us.

It soon becomes debatable whether soft beach sand or sticky clay on the track leading up to Pukekowhai Point is the harder to walk on. The clay is just wet enough to stick to our boots so that the soles soon resemble dinner plates. It is particularly tiring for my eight-year-old companion and it is with some relief that we reach the ridgetop and begin our descent to Anawhata.

This area contains a maze of inland tracks but we stick close to the coast, following then crossing Cannibal Creek. We can see the fast party on the other side of the Anawhata Stream, beginning the long climb to the heights of Anawhata Road. We elect to break right for the beach with a lunch stop in the dunes. We have been on the trail for nearly 6 hours and are about halfway. A food and drink stop of reasonable length is a great reviver and we set off with fresh enthusiasm for the long haul out of Anawhata.

I am told that a youthful Mr Bethell used to catch a ferry to Whatipu on a Friday night, walk to his farm at Te Henga, work all weekend, and walk back on Sunday afternoon for the ferry back to Auckland. Those must have been the days. The timbermen put a tramline on this impossible gradient we are sweating up and then had it plummeting down to Piha, which was the centre of a thriving timber industry.

The chance to ride this route on top of a log hauler has long since gone so we head down the well-used White Track and through an ethereal nikau grove to Piha. There are at least two good reasons for being at Piha. The first is that the La Roche family have a bach there and Pat, who is with our group and whose two sons have run on to Whatipu – has arranged to have the kettle boiling. The second is that mother is waiting for my young companion, who has put in a sterling hour for each of her eight years.

The rest of us grab our packs and motor up the Piha hill, the fast party and Whatipu in our sights. On this tramp what goes up must come down. We head for sea level, this time around Mercer Bay and down the Ahu Ahu Track to Karekare.

Fishermen on the rocks south of Karekare tell us that the tail-enders of the fast

adventure log

GETTING THERE: The entrance to the Te Henga Walkway is off Constable Road, near Muriwai. You can exit at Bethells Beach, Piha or Karekare, or carry on to Whatipu, near Huia.

WALKING TIME: Around 11 hours for the entire trek but the day can be tailored to suit. A long but easy walk – or run.

MAP: LINZ Q11 & Pt R11; Waitakere Ranges Regional Parkland Recreation and Track Guide.

FURTHER INFORMATION: Consult AA GUIDE TO NORTH ISLAND WALKWAYS, WAITAKERE WALKS by Graeme Foster and WALKING THE WAITAKERE RANGES by Alison Dench and Lee-anne Parore. ARC info from ParksLine 0-9-303 1530.

party are about 20 minutes in front of us. The tide is fairly high but there is still plenty of light to negotiate the rocks the tide sometimes sweeps over, which still contain some rusty spikes from the timber tramline.

There are two ways to make the nearly two-hour walk to the road-end at Whatipu. If you follow the shoreline sand you avoid climbing up and down sand dunes. But in recent years the sand has extended several kilometres seaward where the beach nears the Manukau Harbour entrance. That means a long walk across the sand to Whatipu. The alternative is to hug the land; but that means negotiating extensive swamp areas where streams run off into the sand hills.

We choose the most direct, inland route. The old tramline is around here somewhere but is lost in the dunes, marsh and failing light. We wade through the Pararaha Stream in midwinter darkness and find the old vehicle track that is the easy, if sometimes flooded, route to the end of our journey.

There is enough light in the moon to make torches barely necessary. When we reach the Whatipu car park we have been on the trail for over 11 hours. We have walked down one of the most rugged coasts in the country, along ironsand beaches, through temperate rain forest, around volcanic cliffs and along a historic tramline. We have been on exposed headlands and in sheltered valleys. We have been a little mad in the middle of winter. But chances are, we will do it again next year.

cockies among the kauri

The incongruity is palpable. It is Waitangi Day and most of the nation is at play yet in more than an hour only one person has crossed our path. We are surrounded by thick bush and giant kauri that somehow escaped last century's pillaging. Yet the city hewn from the bushmen's plunder – the largest in the country – is just a comfortable commuter trip away. The roar of an airliner, heard but unseen, and the clatter of a helicopter are occasional reminders that civilisation is only out of sight.

Most bizarre of all is the deafening caterwauling and screeching that comes from the bush ahead. We have been on the lookout for a flock of kaka often found in these parts, but when we finally pinpoint the source of the racket it is another parrot altogether. High in the spreading tops of one of the largest kauri are at least five sulphur-crested cockatoos, rising to wheel and squawk among the branches for a few minutes before settling down for a brief spell of silence.

It doesn't seem possible; the last time I saw one of these birds was in a eucalypt tree in their native Australia. But a check through field glasses confirms that a Waitakere Ranges kauri makes just as satisfactory a perch for a cockatoo. While some may be escaped caged birds there is good reason to believe that a few have been blown across the Tasman on their own wings. It must be a good day for birds because we have already seen several eastern rosellas, heard the song and rustle of tui and, before our tramp began, passed beneath three fat kereru (native pigeons) sitting lordly on telegraph wires.

It is also a good day for a tramp that has been sitting around on the 'must do' list for some time. The route from the Waitakere Golf Course to Te Henga/Bethells Beach is occasionally on tramping-club trip programmes but is largely unknown to the public because it detours from named and formed tracks. It is best done with another family so that one car can be taken to the beach and another left in the Cascade Kauri car park at the start of the tramp.

The Cascades area is a popular family picnic spot with lots of space for play and the clear waters of the Waitakere Stream at hand to cool off in. Thanks to the foresight of the Auckland City Council, with help from the government of the day, the virgin kauri forests in the area were bought as a reserve in 1926 and thus saved from the rapacious saws of the Kauri Timber Company.

The reserve is now part of the Centennial Memorial Park and is managed by the Auckland Regional Council. A particular feature of the area is the Cascade gorge where water from the Cascade Stream thunders over a huge cataract. A delightful loop trail peppered with informative signs leads past several giant, venerable kauri.

The loop walk is a circuitous way to begin our tramp but it is too interesting to miss and gives us an easy beginning to the day. The tramping takes on a more serious note when we branch off onto the Upper Kauri Track. My wife, who was persuaded to come on the grounds that it is a three-hour, all downhill walk, is none too impressed as we start climbing a ridge away from the Waitakere Stream. It is true it is downhill to our sea-level destination; I just forgot to mention that the stands of virgin kauri we are passing through clothe a rugged landscape and we will have to climb a few ridges on the way.

We turn onto the Lower Kauri Track and sometimes from the ridges can look across the bush tops to the golf course, where the early-morning players seek birdies of a different sort. Morning tea is taken near the kauri with its noisy Australian house guests. If there is any disappointment in this odd sight it is only that the tree is so large that the cockies are too far away to really admire.

Nonetheless, the bush and the solitude as we trek on are something to luxuriate in. At the Wainamu Stream the track heads south until it joins with several others and makes its way to Te Henga/Bethells Beach by a variety of routes. We are taking what tramping clubs call the 'wet' route, following the Wainamu Stream until it runs into Lake Wainamu and then on down through the inland dunes to the beach.

We head off down the easy-going stream but it soon becomes obvious that enough trampers have followed this route to make a discernible trail on the stream bank. It is possible to walk much of the way without getting wet feet except at times to cross to the other bank. As the walk time passes 4 hours that concession is probably just as well – at least until the inevitable happens. Somewhere ahead is the unmistakable roar of a waterfall.

When we reach the source of the noise we find it is more in the nature of a series of huge boulders. Not all the party are happy, but it is quite easy to sidle around the obstacle. The difficulty comes when we are confronted by a

20m-long pool through a narrow, rock-walled gorge. It would be possible to back-track slightly and climb up and around the problem, but in this heat we opt for a quick swim.

Soon the valley begins to open out, and the water in the stream becomes more languid and the stream edges covered in water weed. Just above where the stream falls into the swampy upper reaches of Lake Wainamu we meet our first picnickers. We are still 50 minutes or so from our car but it is easy walking beside the lake. So many people are playing on the dunes that we imagine it must be an organised party. But it is just a public-holiday crowd enjoying the unusual opportunity to ride a board down a sand dune into a freshwater lake.

We have been on the trail for nearly 6 hours when we reach the west coast surf, a crowded beach and swimmers jammed between guarded flags. Okay, it did take longer than imagined. The penalty is an order to buy takeaways for tea. But that is a small price to pay to get so far from a madding holiday crowd without really leaving it. The cockatoos excepted, of course.

hidden delights on the shore

Bob Ussher is a walking encyclopedia of the outdoors. Make that tramping and climbing. This stalwart of the Alpine Sports Club, of which he has had a long and esteemed period as president, has not only spent a lifetime in the New Zealand outdoors, but along the way has collected so much information about people and places that it should be bottled before it is lost.

It was Ussher who back in 1967 wondered why New Zealand, with all its 'paper' roads drawn by desk-bound cartographers, shouldn't have a public walkway system to equal the ancient bridle paths of Britain. The result of his wondering was an ASC-inspired initiative by the Federated Mountain Clubs that led to the New Zealand Walkways network and an Act of Parliament that envisaged walking tracks throughout New Zealand and stretching from North Cape to Bluff.

The quango killing of the 1980s put an end to the Walkways Commission and dealt a blow to Ussher's dream of a broad network of walking trails suited to general walkers, not just experienced trampers. But before the impetus was lost we did manage to get one delightful coast and bush walkway near Auckland firmly established.

I say 'we' because Ussher gives me credit for a crucial section of the walk, although I doubt the credit is deserved. The accolade arose because the former Lands and Survey Department's publicity on the fledgling Okura Bush Walkway, from Haigh Access Road at Okura to Stillwater on the Weiti River, had preceded completion of the track.

With a couple of young children in tow, I had set off for a day walk relatively close to home – only to find that the promised bridge across the Okura River was nothing more than an item on a government official's wish list. I wrote a story anyway, referring to the bridge as the nowhere bridge, Auckland's answer to the famous Whanganui edifice. Some time later the bridge was duly built and in a story in the ASC bulletin Ussher gave me the credit. It's humbling that he still refers to the wooden footbridge that crosses the Okura River as the Colin Moore bridge.

Fortunately, there is no sign to that effect, so it can remain as an urban, or ASC, myth. But this is one walkway for which DOC, with its limited resources, has given time and money, and Joe Scott-Woods and I decide it is worth checking out the result.

Across the footbridge, where we pause to watch a pied shag fishing for smelt and bullies in the Okura River, the track through the Okura Bush Scenic Reserve has been widened and benched through the coastal nikau forest. In its early days this was a steep and muddy section, but now the standard is such that we share our walk with the training efforts of several multisporters and harriers.

Along the path DOC has labelled many of the trees and shrubs, including the smaller, nondescript species that don't usually get a mention. Their identification is a particularly nice touch on the walk. There are several large kauri in the reserve but Joe leads me to one magnificent specimen slightly off the trail that had been pointed out to him by Bob Ussher. I deem it shall henceforth be known as the Bob Ussher kauri.

The track drops down onto the shelly foreshore of Karepiro Bay, where a Sydney gentleman farmer, Ranulf Dacre, built a one-room brick cottage in the 1850s. Dacre Cottage was in ruins until 1963, when the Historic Places Trust found and restored it. The cottage is now decorated in the style of the 1800s and can be rented by trust members. The extensive pasture flats behind, now grazed by horses, were cultivated by Maori gardeners who settled on the headlands on either side of the valley.

We take advantage of the low tide to walk around the foreshore to Stillwater and the Weiti River. One-way walkers could organise a shuttle to the end of Deep Creek Road but we retrace our steps, this time climbing over the headland and along the cliff with its extensive view of the bay.

On the tidal flats and the shell bank that protects the entrance to the Okura River numerous wading birds are collecting lunch. Karepiro Bay and the Okura

River are included in the Long Bay-Okura Marine Reserve and, with all fish and shellfish totally protected, the sandy shores, rocky reefs, estuarine mudflats and mangrove reaches will in time attract larger numbers of birds.

The coastal walk from Long Bay reaches the headland opposite Dacre Point, and the adventurous, who time the tides and don't mind mud on the boots, could probably make a major trip of it and walk the edge of the marine reserve from Toroa Point at Torbay to Stillwater.

Perhaps I can get Bob Ussher to lead it.

a dam so near and yet so far

The item in the *New Zealand Herald* of 22 January 1904 is as brief as it is intriguing. The paper's Whangaroa, Northland, correspondent reports by telegraph that the *Ngapuhi* excursionists are delighted with Whangaroa Harbour but unfortunately drizzling rain has interfered with picnics that had been arranged.

'Notwithstanding the adverse conditions a small party has set out on horseback to the bush to witness the tripping of a timber dam, which had been specially arranged for the occasion. Few outside of the ordinary timber workers ever have an opportunity of seeing such a unique sight.'

Historian David Johnson, who kindly provided a copy of the *Herald* report, noted such incidents in his book *Summer Cruise, Being the Grand Pleasure Trip of the s.s. Ngapuhi along the northern coast of New Zealand*. His descriptions of densely wooded bush, tall kauri, hills cut by steep gullies, streams tumbling towards the harbour and the tripping of a monster timber dam set the imagination racing. The dam was 'two and a half miles from the timber booms at the head of the harbour and five miles by squelching, muddy track from Totara North,' he wrote. And to watch the tripping of it was considered the high point of the *Ngapuhi* cruise.

The densely wooded bush and tall kauri have long since gone from Whangaroa but the gullies and streams remain – and maybe some evidence of a timber dam too. So we study the map and the late E.V. Sale's history of Whangaroa County for some clues. An illustration shows a newly built driving dam in 'Campbell's Bush, behind Totara North' and says that when it is tripped the logs will be taken into the Whangaroa Harbour at Wairakau and towed from there to Lane's Mill at Totara North, where some would be used by Lane and Brown's shipyard. It was the largest in Australasia and built some of the finest sailing ships to come out of New Zealand.

The Wairakau Stream, which meanders through mangroves into the head of the western arm of the harbour, is familiar territory to us and most

Mokoroa Stream in Goldie Bush, Waitakere Ranges – a place to be shared with friends. (Joe Scott-Woods)

Poley Bay on the tip of the Coromandel Peninsula, where the views of the Hauraki Gulf are extensive and dolphins play in the surf.

The rugged West Coast from the Te Henga Walkway: O'Neill Bay, Erangi Point, Ihumoana Island and Te Henga/Bethells Beach and beyond.

Te Muri Beach, Mahurangi, where the sunrise invites a sea kayaker to spend another day on the Hauraki Gulf.

Little Tree, *a wood strip Canadian canoe beautifully crafted from native timber, wets her bottom on the Waikato River at Tuakau.*

A solo canoeist paddles down the Whanganui River on the country's premier voyage for open canoes.

A waterfall hidden in Lucas Creek, in the heart of suburban Albany, brings a magical kayak journey to an end.

Navigating the weed-infested Kaipara River, near Helensville, a journey that pioneering settlers called 'purgatory'. Modern adventurers demented enough to retrace the Portage between the Waitemata and Kaipara Harbours will fully concur.

Whangaroa boaties. Beyond the mangroves, where the stream narrows into a spectacular rock canyon, is the deepest and coolest of swimming holes.

Yachties come here to get the salt out of their hair. But not far beyond this magic pool the walking track to Totara North branches off over ridge and gully and the rest of the stream is virgin country just waiting to be explored. In the main, the Wairakau is one of those streams that are a delight in the New Zealand bush. There are lazy pools, short boulder-strewn reaches and overhanging ferns. And because this is Whangaroa there are places where the remnants of volcanoes that erupted 20 million years ago rise up in cliffs that appear to be made of exposed aggregate concrete.

With each step we climb higher into the range and there are more and more narrow places that seem likely dam sites. The steep sides of the stream, the depth of the pools and the huge boulders force us away from the stream several times and we must be careful not to lose sight of it. In this country it would be quite easy to move into another catchment without realising it.

By mid-afternoon we reach an impressive waterfall. It is in three sections, each about 10m high. Half an hour later we come to an almost identical cascade. We learn later that this is the spot where Stefano and Lindsay of the nearby Kahoe Farms backpacker lodge sometimes take their guests on a hike past 'historic kauri dams' and to 'bathe in natural rock pools beneath cascading waterfalls'. The only real evidence of the dams, Stefano tells me, is where the water has carved a deep pool when the dam was tripped.

So on another expedition we return to the 1148ha Mangonui State Forest and head up the Tahuna Stream, a tributary of the Wairakau that penetrates far deeper into the forest. Kauri dam remains are the excuse for the expedition but there is much more to it than that. The best sort of tramping is over trackless country using streams as a highway into the interior. And so much the better when it is a confined region that theoretically you cannot be lost for long in, and when you can sit and plan it like an expedition in search of lost treasure.

It is in the nature of stream bashing that you take the long road. In places floods have left convenient flats beside the stream that make for easy walking. Elsewhere there is no alternative but to clamber up into the bush. And sometimes the easiest route is in the bed of the boulder-strewn stream.

At length we reach a tight hairpin that seems to coincide with the map. From now on we must count streams on our right and streams on our left so that we will know which branch in the headwaters to follow to reach a saddle that will lead us out of the bush to farmland.

The difficulty is to decide which streams are shown on the map and which are not. Size should give a clue but it is by no means an infallible guide because uneven rainfall may mean that a lesser stream is carrying more water at the time you reach it. And from the air the streams give an impression quite different from the one the mapmakers would have got had they been on foot.

This is where a sixth sense could come in handy because when you can't see any landmarks a map is not much help, and all my compass does is confirm I am on the right bearing. Given these riven ranges I could have followed an errant creek into a different catchment.

Eventually our stream branches just as it is supposed to. The gully narrows and across the stream is a squared log, about 400mm square and 5m long. At first I imagine it is one of the thousands of kauri logs that never reached the harbour booms but were stranded and left to rot in the bush. Perhaps floods have jammed it across the stream and rasped it into shape.

It is my daughter who points out that nature doesn't put railroad spikes into timber. We have found our eldorado: the log with rusty steel spikes along its length was surely part of the trip mechanism for a timber dam.

All that is left to complete our expedition is to sidle up out of the stream, cross the saddle and make our way home. An hour or so later we reach the top of a ridge and spot the saddle in the distance. To get there we must negotiate a series of steep gullies and it slowly begins to sink in: we have made the classic error of climbing out of the main stream too early. We have travelled across rough country that we had planned to traverse in a stream-bed.

We finally reach farm paddocks $11^1/_2$ hours after setting out for the day. The children sing but I am too tired to join them and when we reach the farmhouse I swallow my pride and hitch the last few kilometres home.

A week later my son buys me a present. It is a poster that reads: 'Beaten paths are for beaten men'.

bush meets land from sea

West coast harbour headlands are by nature rugged spots but none more so than Whatipu, at the northern head of the Manukau Harbour. Here bush-clad hills plummet into the harbour or the broad sandy fringe of coastline.

The European settlers who plundered the ranges north of Whatipu for kauri timber hauled the spoils down the coast by steam train to a wharf cut into the rock at Paratutae Island, just inside the harbour entrance at Whatipu. The wharf was sheltered, but getting there was anything but easy for the sailing ships that came to pick up the huge logs. They had to run the gauntlet of a treacherous harbour bar that has claimed many ships, including HMS *Orpheus* in 1863 with the loss of 189 lives.

It is the bush and the sea that draw us to spend a day out at Whatipu, getting a bit of winter mud on our boots and a salt-laden wind blowing the city cobwebs out of our hair. There is another reason, too. Since the last time I visited, Whatipu, including about 6km of rugged coastline and 800ha of sandflats at the mouth of the Manukau Harbour, has been vested in the Auckland Regional Council, after two years of negotiations with the Crown, to become part of the regional park network. The land had been unallocated Crown land and the council its de facto manager for the past 20 years. The council is planning a major planting programme in the area and to upgrade the historic Whatipu Lodge.

The lodge, built in 1867, is just one of the historic features at the remote beach. There is also a series of caves, some so large they were used last century for socials – one even had a wooden dance floor.

Most of Whatipu beach did not exist before 1900. A 1km strip of sandflats between the cliffs and the sea formed in about 30 years, much to the delight of the endangered dotterels and variable oystercatchers that nest on the wetlands. But for this trip we head inland on the Kura Track, following the Whatipu Stream up the valley where several fortified pa once commanded the high points. From here Te Kawerau a Maki, the tribe of the ranges, could

GETTING THERE: From Huia follow the gravel Whatipu Road to its end.

WALKING TIME: While you could easily complete the route in a morning – or an afternoon – to do so would be a waste. Plan on a day in the outdoors.

MAP: LINZ Q11 & Pt R11; Waitakere Ranges Regional Parkland Recreation and Track Guide.

FURTHER INFORMATION: Consult AA GUIDE TO NORTH ISLAND WALKWAYS, WAITAKERE WALKS by Graeme Foster and WALKING THE WAITAKERE RANGES by Alison Dench and Lee-anne Parore. This is a colonial museum you are trekking through, so to fully appreciate the area it is necessary to research its fascinating history. A starting point may be HUIA, AN ALBUM FROM THE PAST, Lodestar Press. ARC info from ParksLine 0-9-303 1530.

watch for invading Ngati Whatua or Ngapuhi.

Our mission is peaceful and so is the stream, which is more in the nature of a babbling brook. Past floods have deposited large boulders at convenient points so that with care we can cross the stream with dry feet. Eventually the trail climbs towards the Puriri Ridge Track on the southern ridge, but first we want to continue upstream to where, we have been told, there is a waterfall worth seeing.

We pass a small stream coming down Rimu Gully and then turn in to Jones Stream. Now there are large boulders to clamber over and the stream is flanked by cliff faces that are too steep and rocky for vegetation. More scrambling and there is the waterfall, although it is actually a series of cascades, the last one being virtually impassable. At the foot of each cascade is a deep pool that in the height of summer would bring a welcome relief.

Back on the Kura Track the trail climbs a set of reasonably gentle switchbacks until it reaches the ridge and a junction with the Puriri Ridge Track. Head north and this will take you to Mt Donald McLean and panoramic views of Auckland city, the southern Waitakere Ranges and the Manukau Harbour.

Our destination is back to our Whatipu starting point and we turn south to Whatipu Road and the start of the Puriri Ridge Track and, across the road, the end of the 3km Omanawanui Track. It may not be far, but the estimated walk time of 2 hours 15 minutes is not overly generous.

On our left at the beginning of the track is Destruction Gully, where Te Kawerau a Maki suffered heavy losses in a battle with Ngati Whatua. There is an element of frustration in the route ahead because Wonga Wonga Bay, just inside Paratutae Island, seems almost at our feet on one side of the ridge, and Whatipu and the car park where we left our car, on the other.

First we have to climb Omanawanui's 241m, twice drop about 100m and then climb it again before reaching the last trig marker. The rewards for our efforts are stunning views of the Manukau Harbour entrance, South Head, the Awhitu Peninsula on the southern shore, the site of the old wharf and the accretive sands of Whatipu – west coast bush and beach at its best.

paddling pleasures

Sea kayaks and canoes were used to hunt food and explore the wilderness. Modern adventurers paddle their way to quiet bays on the coast, explore sea caves, follow rivers into the bush and get back to the basics of water travel.

beating the urban grind

It is an otherwise dismal Saturday morning. The junior girls' hockey has been cancelled because of the overnight drizzle and most parents are listening to the radio in fervent hope that other children's sports will follow suit.

A few joggers are out along the Auckland waterfront under the protection of thin nylon parkas. And one baby, nestling under the hood of a trendy three-wheeled pushchair, is speeding along pushed by one of those super-healthy, super-beautiful couples. At St Heliers there is a bunch of redoubtable trampers from the Alpine Sports Club. They have neither boots nor packs but hover over a fleet of colourful sea kayaks.

Most tramping clubs tend to be eclectic about outdoor pursuits and Alpine Sports, the largest in the country, is no exception. Since it was formed in 1929 by an informal group of trampers, it has encouraged a love of the outdoors – whether mountain, river, forest or coast.

Outdoors enthusiast Joe Scott-Woods is leading club members on a tramp in the inner Hauraki Gulf. Two have succumbed to the weather but we still number 21, including John Dobbie, a master craftsman of wooden kayaks visiting from Nelson, and kayaking guru Peter Sommerhalder, who has hired out many of the craft these mostly novice paddlers are using.

In the 1860s the founder of modern canoeing, John MacGregor, made a series of remarkable long-distance voyages on European waterways and in the Baltic Sea in his decked canoe, *Rob Roy*. In this country most kayaks disappeared down the foaming water of river rapids but, in the wake of a sea-kayaking revival in North America, they have returned to the sea here too.

The modern sea kayak has evolved from the traditional and extremely seaworthy Eskimo hunting kayaks. They are long, roomy and stable, with watertight bulkheads and waterproof gear stowage compartments. As with the sailing dinghy cruiser – and sea kayaks can be rigged with a small sprit sail or parafoil kite for sailing off the wind – the craft is like a giant pack frame carrying an adventurer's gear. In fact, sea kayaking is more akin to tramping or mountaineering than whitewater canoeing. Sea kayakers go places free of rules or restrictions other than those imposed by the sea. Their boat is a means, not an end in itself.

At last the group is ready. After safety instructions from Sommerhalder and Scott-Woods it launches into the grey waters of the Waitemata. There is an easterly blowing that is enough to warrant using a paddle jacket for warmth but not so strong as to cause any paddling problems.

Browns Island is underfoot within an hour. Scott-Woods calls the distinctive volcanic island Auckland's Taj Mahal. That may be a little extravagant but the land's silhouette is certainly one that ought never to be compromised. The trampers pay homage by climbing to the top of the cone, from where they can see that they are not the only ones unfazed by greyness of the morning. It may be no good for junior hockey but this is fishing weather and Motuihe Channel has its usual fleet of hopefuls. On the beach as we have a morning snack we can hear the dull roar of the city. At first it sounds to me like a large ship is heading our way but there is nothing in sight. It is the combined background noise of urban traffic.

Sommerhalder delivers a timely reminder to keep in a group. We are heading into ferry waters. As colourful as they might be, the sea kayaks are difficult for a high-speed ferry to spot. If we are not careful we could be as vulnerable as a bush-bashing tramper in the middle of the deer roar.

Our island hopping is uneventful and we glide under the Motuihe wharf on a glassy sea that the island protects from the easterly wind. Our timing is perfect. Just as we unpack lunch and make for the substantial wooden day shelter and toilet block on the island park, down comes the rain. The torrential downpour is over by the time we are ready for the last leg across the channel to Home Bay on Motutapu Island.

The fishermen tell us the fishing is okay, but the only fish I see landed is clearly under-sized. The extensive paddock that is the camping ground at Home Bay is deserted. The ground has a water supply and clean toilets, maintained by DOC.

There is time to swim, to try out different kayak designs and to say hello to *Seventh Heaven*, a luxury launch anchored in the bay. Sharing the bay too is the *Pelican*, a beautiful navy blue ketch from Copenhagen. Its bright anchor warp is reflected in its gleaming hull. By coincidence a 15-strong group of sea kayakers on a tour organised by the Auckland Canoe Club is on a similar voyage and paddles in to Home Bay for the night. It is beginning to sound like a sea kayakers' convention as we sit in the dark stirring billies outside hikers'

adventure log

GETTING THERE: Anywhere from St Heliers to Takapuna gives sea kayakers ready access to the inner Hauraki Gulf. Choose a departure point that best suits your route, your shuttle drivers and the weather.

PADDLING TIME: How long is a piece of string? An hour or a week. It's up to you.

MAP: LINZ R10, R11

MARINE CHART: 5324

FURTHER INFORMATION: Join a commercial adventure – there are several operators including Auckland Wilderness Kayaking 0-9-813 3399, www.nzkayak.co.nz – or club trip. For Motutapu Island information consult DOC 0-9-307 9279.

tents, discussing kayaks and kayak design.

It rains in the night but next morning the promised improvement in the weather arrives. As we paddle out of the bay we wake the crew of the *Pelican* and three teenagers who have arrived in the night on a small sloop and are having potato crisps and a bottle of beer for breakfast.

There are some nifty 'rock gardens' along the coast so the daring among us decide to paddle through the gaps. As we pass Station Bay and around into the Rakino Channel there is a slight swell that helps the kayaks to surge through the slots. When there is this much fun to be had around the reefs there doesn't seem much point in paddling in a straight line.

Around Billy Goat Point and on to Administration Bay, where we stop for a snack and to greet Hilary Iles, who with husband George is a resident teacher at the island's outdoor education camp. The last time I was here it was with a school party planting pohutukawa seedlings grown in the island nursery. But the stately pohutukawa between Administration Bay and Gardiners Gap, which separates Motutapu from Rangitoto, are a sorry sight when seen from a kayak. Most are dead or just struggling to survive. Anyone who campaigns against a 1080 blitz against possums should be made to paddle along this stretch of coast. I wonder what will happen to our carefully planted trees unless these destructive marsupials are annihilated.

It is near high tide and mullet dart beneath the kayak hull as we glide through the shallow and still waters of the gap. A cloud of silt indicates where a flounder has been disturbed. By paddling under the causeway bridge we arrive in Islington Bay and have all but circumnavigated Motutapu. To honour our voyage there is bright sunlight in time for lunch. Islington Bay is mirror calm and out in the Motukorea Channel the yachts head back to Half Moon Bay with a little help from their engines.

In these conditions a sea kayak bowls along at a hearty jog without too much effort and we paddle from 'Izzy Bay' to St Heliers comfortably in 85 minutes.

'Looks like you have to be fit for that,' says one Sunday walker as he passes me on St Heliers Beach.

'Or mad,' I reply.

It's not true. It's no more arduous than a brisk walk and anyone who escapes the city for a weekend tramping trip without actually leaving it can hardly be mad. But then we don't really want to tell too many people that. There is a limit to how many kayaks you can fit on Home Bay beach.

golden times on the river

Sometime in the 19th century it is possible that someone breasted the Coromandel Range about where the present Kopu–Hikuai road lies and muttered something like: 'There's gold in them thar hills – and water too.' For there was a river running through the hills carrying precious water, essential to extract the quartz-trapped ore discovered at Broken Hills in 1893.

Downstream from the gold mines the Tairua River emerges into the estuarine expanse of the Tairua Harbour, a front-door playground for Tairua and a sheltered boat haven for the Pauanui Beach resort. A century ago the harbour was filled with a floating carpet of kauri logs that the river and the many streams that feed it flushed out of the Coromandel hinterland. But the gold-miners and kauri bushmen probably never dreamed that the river might also be used as a source of fun and adventure.

Modern kayakers and anglers know differently. In its upper reaches the Tairua runs through some of the most dramatic scenery on the Coromandel Peninsula. This is a land rent by volcanic explosion, glaciation, erosion and rising and falling sea levels. Craggy bluffs, created by erosion, and massive lava columns formed seven or eight million years ago overlook the river. Behind them are crevasse-like valleys and imposing bush-clad peaks. Set against this rugged grandeur the river seems almost civilised. At normal flow it is more romantic than cavalier, its rapids frequent but non-threatening. The water tends to tumble more than gallop, often over quite shallow reaches.

The Tairua has another feature. While its headwaters lie in some of the more inaccessible places in the range, it flows under the Kopu–Hikuai highway just below the Fourth Branch, a major tributary. Then it takes a wide semi-circular sweep before coming back to touch the highway again at the turn-off to Pauanui and below the First Branch. Between the Fourth and First Branches of the Tairua River lies some of the most impressive scenery in the Coromandel.

There can hardly be a more agreeable place to introduce mainly novices to whitewater kayaking – which is exactly what eclectic outdoorsman Joe Scott-

Woods does in organising a weekend river adventure for the Alpine Sports Club. What the Tairua lacks in water – and the river is even lower this year than normal – it makes up for with its convenience. Between the two major highway bridges is DOC's Broken Hills campground. It is a pleasant, basic site with grassy, sheltered terraces and pit toilets. The clear Tairua is an on-site water supply.

It seems fitting that this adventure should have a relatively easy start and we meet at the campground at 11am. At least it is easy for us. Our instructors from Outdoor Addictions, who come with hired river kayaks, arrived in the dark the night before and were up at 7am to run the river. Chief kayak instructor Jonathan Iles has taped to his foredeck a detailed plan of the river that he has surveyed. Every likely problem that might be encountered is marked.

After pitching our tents and grabbing a bite to eat, we sit down for a briefing. Iles, a former army officer and policeman, keeps it brief too. He tells us to always keep pointing downstream and that if we are lodged on a rock to 'hug the rock' and lean downstream. That way the water will bubble under the hull and free us. Leaning upstream is almost certain to end in capsize.

On the river bank beside the first highway bridge the group members are assigned their kayaks and given some instruction in safety signals. Then in a large pool before the first rapid we are broken into three small groups, each with an instructor, and practise basic forward and back strokes and sweep strokes.

Several of the group, such as Japanese language student Midori Yamada, have never been in any sort of kayak before. It is my first time in a river kayak and I quickly begin to enjoy the experience. The cockpit fits like an O.J. Simpson glove and what the kayak lacks in stability it more than makes up for with the sensation of oneness it imparts. And its manoeuvrability is stunning. Dip the blade in and this machine will spin on its axis.

Therein lies the greatest difficulty for novice river paddlers. These craft are not really designed for straight line running and in a river like the Tairua – where rapids are often separated by lengthy, quiet running pools – there is often a need to paddle a steady course.

Many of the rapids are quite shallow and it is essential that we pick the 'right' line not so much to ensure our safety but to stop the kayak running aground. Iles's briefing before each stretch of whitewater becomes invaluable in helping us stick to the deeper channels. He also warns us of 'strainers'. In river kayaking a strainer is a branch or log sticking out into the water that could cause quite a mess if an incautious paddler was strained through it.

On a couple of the more tricky rapids Iles goes ahead and waits to give assistance to anyone who might capsize. No one does but sometimes he has to rescue people who have become stranded on a large boulder. One of the interesting outcomes is that the first-time paddlers generally seem to handle their kayaks better through the rapids than on flat water. It probably has something to do with the water flow and the design of their craft.

Next morning we wake to a soft frost around our tents. While we still lie snug in our sacks Iles and his guides are off checking out the second half of our journey. The rest of us check out the old mine sites. Nature has restored the land to leafy beauty but evidence of the miners' labours remains in the shafts dug by hand deep into the hills. In 30 years of sweat and toil some 1.7 tonnes of bullion was won from 37,000 tonnes of quartz. Now glow-worms and cave weta inhabit the tunnels.

Back at the camp we prepare for the second half of the journey. Iles estimates it will take about $3^1/_2$ hours. After the first half hour, where we stop for a soup break, the rapids become less frequent and there are long, lazy pools to test our straight-line paddling skills.

It has been a non-threatening entry to the exciting world of whitewater kayaking. We have not found gold but the Tairua River has left us with the riches of new outdoor skills and the memory of a superb weekend.

paddling around the gulf

If the best-laid plans of mice and sea kayakers are not to go astray they at least need to be flexible. So I concluded as I battled up the Rangitoto Channel during the opening hours of a week-long sea kayaking expedition in the Hauraki Gulf.

As car roof-racks around town and secluded bays in the Hauraki Gulf can attest, sea kayaking must be one of the fastest-growing leisure pursuits. It is easy on the joints, not too hard on the pockets and ideally suited to many parts of New Zealand. In the Abel Tasman and Marlborough Sounds areas about 300 sea kayak seats, in singles and doubles, await tourists. A similar surge in tourist fleets has occurred in the Hauraki Gulf and the Bay of Islands.

Recreation doesn't seem to have a high priority in the 30,000ha Auckland conservancy of the Department of Conservation, at least in contrast with other conservancies in the country. It seems that the primary emphasis of DOC's operational role in Auckland is in conservation rather than recreation. Nonetheless the Auckland region still relies on the Gulf islands, which make up about 75 per cent of the DOC estate in the area for traditional recreational opportunities.

Some 47 of the islands are preserved in the maritime park which, when it was established in 1967, was the first in the country. The boom in sea kayaking may put greater pressure on the department to take more interest in recreation and establish more of the basic but welcome facilities for tramping and camping found in the Marlborough park.

As with most outdoor pursuits, sea kayaking has its share of head-down, backside-up types who measure enjoyment in kilometres travelled without much regard for the scenery, creature comforts or sea conditions. And there are those – count me among them – who cannot understand why anyone would want to paddle in a straight line when the inshore scenery is a fascinating world of towering rock cliffs, swirling canyons of kelp, secret caves and bird life.

An added incentive for a Hauraki Gulf tour was the chance to leave my car in my garage and, after trundling my kayak down to the water on trolley wheels, paddle from the upper Waitemata Harbour and back.

'Tramping on water' in a sea kayak has one major advantage over that on dry land. If you don't take the kitchen sink on board it is probably only because the rest of the family might miss it while you are away. There is certainly no shortage of room in most sea kayak holds for a good supply of food, and wine to wash it down.

So, loaded down with comforts for a week, I set off in darkness to try to get some tidal advantage, at least as far as Kauri Point. Paddling in the dark in the stillness of an estuary is a magical experience. Small fish jump ahead of you to make the only ripples on the water.

It is about 7km from the Greenhithe ramp to Kauri Point and I am there in an hour, which is a good kayak cruising speed of a bit under four knots. Another hour takes me the 6km to Stanley Point. An hour again, nearly another 6km, and I am at the north of Cheltenham Beach and a stop for breakfast.

When I round Takapuna Point and head up the Rangitoto Channel, it is into some increasingly big seas and strong winds. For the next 3 hours I battle wind, tide and some steep Hauraki Gulf slop to make just 11km to Rothesay Bay, where I am to meet my companion, Andy Paterson.

I have been hugging the shore to lessen the effect of the tide but the down side of that policy is having to contend with awkward waves bouncing back off the cliffs. So when Andy suggests we abandon plans to paddle another 14–15km to Te Haruhi Bay and a backpack campsite at Shakespear Regional Park and instead drive to Mahurangi, our next destination, I readily agree.

The best-laid plans need to be flexible.

Te Muri Beach at Mahurangi Regional Park is a short paddle around Cudlip Point – and is a gem of a bay. The weather hasn't improved the next day, so we explore the Mahurangi Harbour and enjoy the solitude of Te Muri. In the evening Andy paddles off Cudlip Point and catches some fish to add to his rations.

Another minor change of plan has us paddling direct for Kawau Island past the small islet of Saddle Island, or Te Haupa, which guards the entrance to the Mahurangi. We are heading for Motutara and Moturekareka islands. At low tide the islands, which now belong to the public, are joined by a sandbar. The 4ha Motutara has been part of the maritime park since its inception. An old quarry, worked during the Depression, has left a crater-shaped arena. Moturekareka has recently been bought by DOC. Its private owners scuttled a hulk in front of their cottage to serve as a breakwater, and cut paths through the scrub to the island's beaches and lookout points.

We stop for lunch at Beehive Island, a tiny knoll surrounded by a ring of brilliant white shells. Ahead is Kawau Island and our marker, the old copper mine chimney. Kawau Island doesn't offer much joy for kayakers – something else DOC might like to consider while it is planting trees and saving birds – but we are fortunate to have the use of a friend's bach at North Cove.

The next day I paddle around to Slater Point on the other side of the island. At secluded Sandy Bay I have a swim and lunch. There is a track there from North Cove and a sign asking people to respect private property.

As a young hitch-hiker I was once picked up by a truck driver who asked if I knew why he had stopped for me and not someone further down the road. It was because I was walking. 'You were doing something so I thought I'd do something for you,' he said.

Ever since, I have believed that effort is deserving of some reward, or at least to be first in line for it. So now that I am paddling a sea kayak I idly think about a sign that might say 'sea kayakers only welcome'. But then I consider the numbers being sold and the size of the tourist fleets and decide it might not be such a good idea, at least not on this secluded beach.

Just across North Channel from where I am sitting is the Tawharanui Regional Park and an isolated backpack campsite that can really only be reached by kayak. We had plans to go there and explore the park but it will have to wait for another trip. I have already decided there are several years of exploring to be done around this coast, so there is no need to be too ambitious on this trip.

From Kawau to Motuora in good conditions proves to be an easy paddle so we arrive in good time, even after spending an hour further exploring Moturekareka.

Andy has to paddle to Mahurangi to retrieve his car but the weather and sea conditions are good so I decide to revert to my original plan and paddle home. It proves to be a bit further and considerably harder than I thought. The 12km run to Huaroa Point at the end of Whangaparaoa is completed in a comfortable 2 hours. But the end of the peninsula is about 3km long. A big swell is bouncing through the Whangaparaoa Passage accompanied by a north-east wind that would drive me on to the rocks if I stopped paddling. I have no alternative but to press on.

In the distance I see something shining and head for it. It is the roof of a house at Campbells Bay, about 15km away. Karapiro Bay is quite indented, so a direct line to my shining roof takes me quite a way out from land and into a horribly large following sea that I am getting too tired to take much advantage of.

I make a thankful land-fall around 2.30pm and get my first rest since setting off at 9am. From here it is a slog down the East Coast Bays, which I vow I will never paddle past again, to North Head. The tide is against me by now so I hug the shore and scoot under the Devonport wharf at about 5pm as the first commuters are coming home.

North Head to Kauri Point is by my reckoning uninspiring paddling, but from there on the harbour is delightful, with bays and bush that Auckland landlubbers would never know existed. The home stretch, which took an hour when I set off, now takes an hour and a half. But considering the tide that is running I think it is a good effort.

The hardest part is yet to come – to push a laden kayak up a steep hill to my home. When I get there it is with an air of quiet satisfaction and the welcome reward of a cold beer.

little tree comes into her own

'Gramma said when you come on something good, first thing to do is share it with whoever you can find; that way, the good spreads out where no telling it will go.' So begins Forrest Carter's *The Education of Little Tree*, the poignant and beautiful tale of a young Native American boy that has been spreading out good since it was published in 1976.

When it came to choosing a name for the 5.3m woodstrip Canadian canoe that Chris Bradbeer and I would paddle for nearly 2300km down Australia's Murray River in November–December 1998, Little Tree, from our family's favourite book, chose itself. A Redbird design along traditional Native American lines, she was beautifully hand-crafted by Nelson canoe and kayak builder John Dobbe from kahikatea – Dobbe says it is more flexible than cedar – with decorative strips of totara, and kauri gunwales.

Throughout our journey *Little Tree* drew admiring looks and comments for her New Zealand timbers and the workmanship of her builder. But since we stepped ashore at Goolwa in South Australia, where the Murray River flows into the Southern Ocean, *Little Tree* has not had her beautiful bottom wet – unless you count being used as a backdrop for a car advertisement. Instead, she has been drawing admiring looks on display at the Auckland Canoe Centre in Sandringham Road, waiting for the right occasion.

Her moment finally comes with a winter tour on the Waikato River with the Auckland Canoe Club, led by the canoe centre owner Peter Sommerhalder. The first part of the trip, from Karapiro to Hamilton, began on a mid-July Sunday. Two weeks later the group paddle on to Ngaruawahia. *Little Tree* and I join them on a third Sunday for the final 25km leg from the bridge at Tuakau to Hoods Landing south of Waiuku.

It is the first time I have been on the river since rowing in regattas at Karapiro, Ngaruawahia and Mercer many years ago. Paddling the 425km Waikato has been on my must-do list for years. I fancy following in the boyhood strokes of New Zealand explorer David Lewis, who kayaked from his boarding school in

Wanganui to his home on Auckland's North Shore using traditional Maori canoe portages at Waiuku and Otahuhu.

Part of the attraction is the huge wealth of history that runs with New Zealand's longest river. It was once a major river road and a valuable source of food. Its waters have carried Maori war canoes and British gunships, driven hydroelectric turbines, charged dairy factory boilers and cooled gas-fired power stations.

The stretch near the river delta has an eccentric contemporary fascination. It is the New Zealand centre for the venerable British Seagull outboard that powered a flotilla to the Normandy landings in the Second World War and the dinghies of New Zealand recreational fishers in the 1950s and 1960s. Every Easter since the mid-1980s the waters of the lower Waikato have been churned by a collection of Seagulls nearing the end of a two-day race from Karapiro. The race gets entries from the United States and Britain. In the open class, souped-up Seagulls on 8m-long skiffs weighing just 30kg reach speeds of up to 40 km/h.

It is a much slower and quieter flotilla that assembles at the Les Batkin Reserve on the river bank near Tuakau. There are 29 sea kayaks, some plastic, some glass fibre, and two of them doubles. And there is *Little Tree*. Sea kayaks are wonderfully versatile recreational craft and are just as practical in a stillwater river such as the Waikato as they are in the sea. But dare I say the open Canadian canoe is even better, although there are precious few rivers in New Zealand that really suit them.

A kayaker says that we look as if we are driving a four-wheel-drive vehicle, an image accentuated by the low sheerline of the Redbird design, and it is a good analogy to the kayakers with their backsides sitting below water level. *Little Tree* is a fast touring canoe with a long water-line and fine entry. Keeping up with a pod of sea kayaks is no problem at all, and from our four-wheel-drive seat there is a grand view of the flax- and willow-lined banks.

The river passes around Kaiwaka No 2 Island and Whatamakiri Island in a large elbow, and we stop for lunch at the Elbow waterski club. Some hardy types pulled by sleek and powerful boats are skiing on this wide stretch of river.

'You lot wouldn't want to be here in the summer,' remarks one speedboat owner in reference to the popularity of the spot with waterskiers. Amen to that.

One boat has four large speakers mounted over the cockpit. Aquatic boom boxes. 'It's great fun skiing to music,' says the young bloke with his head under the engine cowl. 'Except it's not doing anything today because the battery is flat.' And amen to that too.

After the Elbow the river begins to narrow and split as the Aka Aka Stream feeds into it. A newsletter for open canoe enthusiasts calls it the Aka Aka bayou, and to me it evokes images of Huckleberry Finn. Big Jim could well be hiding on one of these tiny willow- and flax-infested islands.

adventure log

GETTING THERE: You can reach the Aka Aka bayou from several landings on the Waikato River between Tuakau and Waiuku – but it is smarter to start upstream.

PADDLING TIME: All day if you want to get the best out of an unusual area.

MAP: LINZ Q12 & R12, R13.

FURTHER INFORMATION: Consult the largest scale map you can find, the locals at the Otaua Tavern and StressFree Adventures, Waiuku. Take care not to miss the Hoods Landing takeout point or you could end up in the Tasman Sea.

Colin Harrington runs StressFree Adventures, an outdoor education company based in Waiuku. He has come along as a volunteer guide and tells us to keep together. If we take a wrong turn we might well get lost or spend a lot of time trying to find our way back to the main channel.

Huck Finn and Tom Sawyer would surely have a ball here, because squatting in the river bank and island thickets are a collection of maimais, motley shacks and some relatively substantial baches, all in various states of repair or disrepair. Most are fronted by a pontoon or crude jetty so the owners can tie up outside their river hideaways.

This is real Kiwi bach country, a place where old timber and corrugated iron, tarpaper and netting are recycled into a holiday home. It's a spot where the river and the world pass by the front door and people make their own entertainment. Road signs and hoardings washed down with the floods are nailed up outside with delightful irreverence.

The floating pontoons have another purpose and some are getting a quick make-over, the shack behind them a tidy-up. The pontoons are used as the platform from which to hang a whitebait net out into the river and tomorrow is the start of the whitebait season. Down on the Aka Aka bayou many of the pontoons have sprouted tarpaulin shelters to keep whitebaiters out of the rain and wind while they wait patiently for the delicacy to arrive. Harrington recalls the days when you could buy a 1kg jar of fresh whitebait at Port Waikato for $1.

There is little environmental purity in the shacks and landings and likely for some the river is a convenient waste drain at the door. Yet the ambience seems somewhat appropriate and the suspicion that a decent 50-year flood would eliminate many of them is reassuring.

Harrington guides us up a side channel hidden behind Motukakaho Island. It is not much larger than a drain, its banks thick with watercress, and opens into a wider reach that leads to Hoods Landing. Sue Sommerhalder is waiting for us with the canoe trailers, hot soup and a sausage sizzle. Under the jetty is an eel head and skin about 1.5m long, and the scallop shells that were probably used to lure it to a waiting line.

At the Otaua Tavern just up the road the locals, whose boat club organises the Seagull races, are playing pool, some singing along with the country music on the jukebox. Photographs on the tavern wall proudly display the catch from various fishing trips.

As Gramma said, when you come on something good, first thing to do is share it with whoever you can find. They understand that down on the Aka Aka bayou.

down the lazy river with me

You can't paddle the Whanganui River on porridge, say the Juice Boys scornfully as they prepare their gargantuan breakfast.

An open fire blazes at the Ramanui Lodge campsite in defiance of the saturation of 24 hours of heavy rain. A 1kg slab of bacon is forked into one blackened pan, a dozen eggs into another and a couple of packets of crumpets, the closest thing to bread left after four days on the river, are toasting on the fringes. A few cans of beer, or 'juice' as the boys call it, complete this real man's breakfast.

My companions look on with a mixture of horror and awe as they tuck in to a typical outdoors breakfast of muesli or porridge and powdered milk or fruit. We came across the Juice Boys, as we dub them, the day before, although unknown to us we have been following them down the Whanganui, gently graded and navigable for 234km, from Taumarunui to Wanganui.

The Whanganui is a pathway through the wilderness, gouged out, Maori legend relates, by Mt Taranaki fleeing to the coast. That water road, from the melting snows of the central North Island mountain trio to the Taranaki coast, has been used by peaceful settlers and invading armies, for food and for spiritual sustenance, to transport trade goods of pounamu and wool bales.

The four likely lads from Paraparaumu had begun their river journey at Taumarunui. Our party from Auckland's Alpine Sports Club put in 58km downstream at Whakahoro, and face a paddle of 87km of wilderness without any road access, before leaving at Pipiriki, 88.5km from the sea.

Some have never paddled an open Canadian canoe before but there are several hundred years of combined outdoors experience among us. Two women in the party are 69, one a club member for 50 years. We have all carried packs through North Island bush and tramped through the alpine foothills of the South Island, boiled a billy beside a good number of streams – and worked out our own preferences for what to carry and what to leave behind.

On our first day the tramping experience doesn't count for much in a

Canadian canoe but our mentor, Peter Sommerhalder of the Auckland Canoe Centre, is there to help us. I am paddling *Little Tree*, my wooden strip canoe, with my eyes glued to the line Sommerhalder is taking through every bend and riffle. I have paddled the Whanganui before, but as forward hand to a highly skilled paddler. Steering my own canoe in anything but flat water is a totally different experience. *Little Tree* is a long and fast expedition canoe, low gunwaled and with a hull designed to be seaworthy in the wind-tossed waves of lake or inshore seas. The back-stopping waves of rapids are not its forte.

The first capsize of our party is before lunch. I might have yahooed but I don't want to tempt fate. It makes no difference. At the next sizeable stretch of white water I follow Sommerhalder into the V of the rapid and the concentration of stopper waves. It is too much for *Little Tree*. The waves spill over the gunwales amidships and we are swamped and over in seconds.

Still, the swamping is part of a steep learning curve. Keep to one side of the larger stopper waves is the obvious lesson. The other is not to disdain the use of a waterproof barrel to carry gear. Kayaking 'dry-bags' don't like to be fully submerged for long periods and I have a lot of gear to dry in the afternoon sun at John Coull Hut.

The terrace where I last camped at John Coull has washed away but a new and fairly expansive camping area has been carved out of the bush. Our hut companions are two Israeli couples. The men are naval officers who have just finished a six-year stint. We manage to talk into the night without discussing Middle East politics. We are thankful that a party of 28 schoolchildren the hut warden is expecting do not reach John Coull.

It starts to rain next morning so we take our morning break under the cooking shelter at the next campsite down-river – and have our first scent of the Juice Boys. The bush and undergrowth are sodden but there are the unmistakable smell and signs of a recent fire. Perhaps they too have heard about the impending arrival of the school party at John Coull.

Their canoes are tied to the river bank at Ramanui when we arrive. They are each towing a tender made from a tractor inner tube with a plywood top and bottom and a hatch to gain access to these aquatic trailers. This is a Likely Lads' holiday. When they left Taumarunui four days earlier their trailers had held 16 dozen cans of beer. Now they are mostly full of empty cans.

Two of the men wear black singlets and bush shirts that suggest they are hunters. And so they are, experienced too. Their paddling skills are probably no better than ours but they have come down-river unscathed, their trailers no doubt acting like drogues.

While we sit in a small shelter cooking our tramping-tack meals over a gas stove, Micky, Pete, Dave and Hutch, outside in the steady rain, cut and chop waterlogged manuka and quickly coax it into a blazing fire on which to cook their sausages, beans and potatoes – Micky never takes a stove into the bush. Lord Baden-Powell says the three Bs of life in camp are the ability to cook bannocks, beans and bacon. You can be sure our friends can. I stand by their fire that night and its heat creates an up-draught that keeps the rain clear of the flames.

Our Israeli friends stay across the river at Tieke Marae. In the morning the river has risen a couple of metres and we wait for them to appear on the bank and see their reaction. Perhaps naval officers don't learn that a log on the Whanganui river bank, no matter how large, is not a good thing to tie a canoe to. Their canoes are about an hour's paddling downstream. Our host at Ramanui has found them on his way to pick up some lodge guests in his jetboat. He takes the embarrassed Israelis downstream and adds salt to the wound with a $60 fee.

At Pipiriki the landing is almost underwater. The Israelis grin sheepishly, the Juice Boys fill a 44-gallon roadside rubbish bin with squashed beer cans – and my paddling partner and I congratulate each other on having learned some new things from three days on the Whanganui River.

At Tieke there is a carved pole that declares the area belongs to the people of Tieke for all time, whether the land is sold, given away or confiscated. If the concept of land never being alienated – regardless of legal circumstance – seems difficult to grasp, paddle down the Whanganui River. Better still, paddle down with the Juice Boys.

around the isthmus

When sea kayaker Laurie Bugbee invites you for a paddle around Auckland, he means it literally. The former health inspector took to sea kayaking as something to do in his retirement and quickly became the father of a pursuit that has grown in Auckland by paddle and stroke.

Bugbee twice set out to paddle from one side of Auckland to the other – the long way, around North Cape – but was thwarted by bad seas and an ill companion. He paddled as far as the Kaipara Harbour on one coast and the Bay of Islands on the other. So when another veteran kayaker Ron Augustin muses on a kayaking circumnavigation of the City of Sails using the old Maori portage routes, Bugbee can't resist.

Better still, decides Bugbee, to do the trip in a day and go anti-clockwise so as to take advantage of the tides.

'Come along in a double, we have a strong, young kayaker to share it with you,' suggests Bugbee.

At 6.20am when we leave St Heliers there is just enough light to make out the time on my watch but barely enough to get a good look at my companions. Damien Milicich, the 'strong young kayaker' is a former judo champion who took to canoeing with the determined enthusiasm of a black belt. Bugbee warns me: 'His only problem is he goes too fast.'

I soon find out what Bugbee means as Milicich's paddle settles into a steady beat. I feel comfortable following the stroke but am glad I do not have to set it. St Heliers disappears behind us and soon Mission Bay and the fountain with its colours is just discernible in the pale dawn. The Friday night storm has gone, there is no wind and the seas are slight – yet we are too early to be run down by the amateur fishing fleet motoring away from the Okahu Bay boat ramp.

As we reach the port two tugs steam towards us. 'Shall we go between them and ride the bow wave,' suggests Milicich, only half joking.

We reach the harbour bridge 10 minutes before eight, our run well inside

Bugbee's estimated 2 hours. A pale sun is just beginning to appear behind Rangitoto and Nancy Augustin calls us back for a group photograph as we pass under the bridge.

Nancy's husband Ron designed the Sea Bear kayaks we are using. The 60-year-old marine engineer and boat designer has been paddling boats of one sort or another since he was four years old and got hooked on canoeing after a Whanganui River trip in 1974. When he reached his fifties he decided he would like to paddle a kayak to Great Barrier Island. As the small river canoes he had designed and built were unsuitable for the trip, he set to and designed the Sea Bear kayak. Since then the Augustins have put in a lot of sea miles in the Hauraki Gulf and Marlborough Sounds, and several hundred other Sea Bears have been built.

More and more outdoor pursuits types are stowing their tramping and mountaineering gear on board a sea kayak and going 'backpacking' on the estuary and coastal waters of the north. The members of my group are no youthful explorers. The average age is well above 40 and Milicich, at 25, is easily the youngest.

Our pod of sea kayaks turns south-west past Watchman Island, through a gap in Meola Reef, and on until we enter the Whau River. But we are going too well and further up the river there will not be enough water yet. So we wait at the boat ramp by the motorway bridge until Laurie's carefully calculated schedule catches up with us.

There is a lot of water in the mangrove-fringed Whau River, and a lot of bird life too. Where the river narrows behind the Avondale racecourse the water is a sickly brown. Past Great North Road factories back on to what is now a narrow creek and there is the unmistakable stench of paint and chemicals. We stop just before a sewer pipe and the rail line block our way, and haul the kayaks out into a firm's backyard in Portage Road, New Lynn. Maori canoeists almost certainly paddled a bit further upstream.

A century ago just 1600m separated the Whau Creek from Green Bay and an enthusiastic Waitemata-Manukau Canal Syndicate survey concluded: 'Unquestionably nature has destined that at some time these rivers shall be the carriers of great commerce.' A report in 1887 by Mr Blair of the Public Works Department was more cautious. 'It seems evident that the work [a canal] is not likely to be taken in hand for some time,' commented the *Auckland Evening Star*.

Obviously Blair did not envisage sea kayaks making the 3.5km portage to the Manukau Harbour on trolleys. Passing motorists also have trouble

GETTING THERE: Start and finish on St Heliers Beach.

PADDLING TIME: A 12- to 14-hour day but can be done in two stages with a stop at Green Bay.

MAP: Any large road map of Auckland.

FURTHER INFORMATION: The circumnavigation was recently run as a two-day event and it may become an annual affair. Contact the Auckland Canoe Centre 0-9-815 2073, www.kayak.co.nz.

envisaging this. 'Which way to St Heliers?' we ask. Their blank stares suggest they think we are mad.

Bugbee stirs us along as we grab a quick coffee: catching the tides is critical. We leave Green Bay at noon with an incoming tide and a strong wind in our favour. The view from a kayak usually provides another perspective and from Green Bay to Onehunga it is certainly different from what we expected. The coastline is an almost unbroken expanse of bush from the skyline to the water's edge.

There is not much green about Westfield, however, when we arrive just after 1pm. We come ashore behind the old Westfield railway station. The mud is black and foul and what appear to be rocks are actually bits of rusted and encrusted machinery and other metal debris.

It is less than 1000m from here to the Tamaki River, and the waters of the Pacific Ocean, as stepped out in 1908 by J.E. Taylor, president of the Manukau-Tamaki Canal Promotion Association.

Maori made extensive use of the narrow portage. They called it Tauomo; it was a bridge on a canoe highway from the Waikato to the North. In the 1850s European settlers put a two-chain canal reserve across the isthmus to connect the Waitemata with the Manukau. In 1860 Colonel Moule, R.E., estimated it would cost £22,876 to dig a suitable canal through it. Blair estimated £550,000.

Undeterred, the Manukau-Tamaki Canal Promotion Association drilled holes across our portage route and concluded from the sand, shell and beach mud brought up each time that the tide had once flowed through the isthmus. Taylor felt it would be possible to dredge right through the isthmus at one-third the cost of the rival Whau scheme and one-sixth that of bridging the Waitemata, 'which would not nearly be so useful as the waterway across the North Island'.

Bugbee seems to have overestimated our paddling time and underestimated our eating time, but he does let us park outside a dairy and have an ice cream, much to the owners' amusement. Every dog in Otahuhu growls at our passing. The locals obviously think we are weird too.

We leave the boat ramp on the Tamaki River behind schedule, but we have the wind and tide with us for the estimated 3 hours it will take to paddle the 18km to St Heliers. It is also familiar country. Every morning as a schoolboy rower I used to train on these waters, when they were free of moored boats and probably a lot cleaner.

When we pass the berth of the giant Sea Tow barge I wonder how it can possibly negotiate the moorings. It obviously succeeds because an hour or so later as we pass Bucklands Beach and head across the river toward Karaka Bay and West Tamaki Head, the barge passes, throwing up a confused sea. The sea is the roughest we have been in all day but it is easily handled in modern sea kayaks.

We pass through a gap in the Achilles Point reef, go past Ladies Bay and arrive at St Heliers beach dead on 6pm. We have circumnavigated a city in a day. My children, who run in the darkness across the beach to greet us, think it a magnificent feat. So do we.

a winter dunking

There should be some reassurance in uncontrollable shivering. It's the body's way of trying to warm up and – as Ian, one of my young companions, reminds me – it's preferable to the listless warmth of advanced hypothermia. But then Ian, who has come to my rescue yet again, is not soaked in freezing Whakatane River water for the umpteenth time and shaking so badly that holding a kayak paddle is utterly impossible.

I have to get warm but every bit of spare clothing is soaked too. Ian drags his dry spares out for me and the shivering subsides as I abandon my kayak and walk about 1km to the Hanamahihi Hut on feet with no feeling – until the bruises come out a few days later.

If I entertained any thoughts that it would have been saner to take this easy riverside trail all the way from Ruatahuna, it is gone by the time I get to the hut where the other mad dogs, and two Englishmen, have the billy boiling. Warmth does wonders for morale and the last people at the hut have considerately left a pile of split firewood that in a few hours will dry out my sleeping bag and clothing.

This historic route through the Urewera National Park to Ruatoki is a popular four-day tramp. Kayaking the 76km should take about half that time and it is not all madness to be going in the middle of winter because in summer there is rarely enough water for kayaks.

According to the late Graham Egarr the Whakatane, with rapids that are no more than grade three, 'is often regarded as an ideal overnight trip for paddlers who are relatively inexperienced at multi-day trips. The rocks tend to well-rounded and the rapids not steep.'

That sounds like us so I prevail on my generous nephew to shuttle our car from Opotiki to Ruatahuna, traditional centre for the Tuhoe people, a place where time has gone backwards and horses outnumber people. The Urewera is different from most national parks in that it contains many pockets of private land, and for much of its length the Whakatane follows a corridor of them.

At Mataatua we get permission from a farmer to portage our kayaks across his paddocks and down a steep fern-covered bank to the river. And here is the way of history. Probably 100km from the coast is the Mataatua Marae where the Mataatua canoe is said to have reached to beget the Tuhoe before journeying to the far north as the founding waka of the Ngapuhi. Joe and Ian have opted to use their solid Puffin sea kayaks.

adventure log

GETTING THERE: The Whakatane River trip begins at Ruatahuna on SH 38 between Murupara and Wairoa. You need to seek the landowner's permission to reach the water.

PADDLING TIME: Allow three days on the river.

MAP: LINZ W16, W17.

FURTHER INFORMATION: There is some useful information in NEW ZEALAND'S NORTH ISLAND RIVERS by Graham Egarr. Consult canoeists in Whakatane and DOC Rotorua 0-7-349 4715, DOC Murupara 0-7-366 5341 or DOC Opotiki 0-7-315 6103.

If the Mataatua can traverse the river, they should be able to as well.

Egarr's description of the first stage as 'easy, shallow grade-one rapids down to Ngahiramai Hut' is mostly accurate, although his idea of a 'steady pace' for river flow is much stronger than I imagined. Anyone trying to cross this river would probably be swept off his or her feet.

As darkness approaches we camp on a river flat where one of the Ruatahuna trekking companies has a huge, canvas-covered kitchen and mess hall that we can cook in if it rains. Next morning I cast a fly line into the water – more to have briefly done it than to actually catch a fish, because it already seems certain that with this party of mostly novices time is going to be precious.

The sun is trying to burn away the Urewera mist and there is no sign of rain. But we move on from the grass and manuka flats to where the dense forest of rimu, matai and totara crowds in on the river and blocks the sun, and the air is instantly colder than a liquor-store chiller.

I call out that I will go ahead and stop behind a larger rapid to take photographs of the rest of the party – and I pay the price for my cockiness. At Tawhiwhi Hut the river narrows and turns abruptly at a cliff face. I slide into the cliff, lean the wrong way and take a swim.

And so begins a chilling day. I wrap around boulders that better skills would easily have avoided, including on the first of the named rapids, Tarakena, which Egarr notes 'contains a large boulder that may be difficult to avoid'. He was right. But I do successfully run Nihootekiore, where the water goes through a narrow gap to create the hardest and most spectacular rapid.

It is brutally cold in a long, gorge-like section of the river and after one spill my kayak disappears several hundred metres downstream before I can retrieve it. The major problem is not falling out but the bitter cold that comes with it. As the day wears on it becomes increasingly debilitating, so when I see the small boulder racing towards me I know what to do but just can't seem to make it work.

Outside Hanamahihi Hut next morning is several degrees of frost. Our spray skirts and dive booties are frozen into distorted sculptures and we have to thaw them in the river before we can get them on. By late morning the river has widened and we catch some warmth. When we reach the road-end at Ruatoki I feel slightly cheated. I haven't had the time to fish for the Whakatane's famed fighting rainbow trout or soak up the atmosphere. This is New Zealand wilderness at its best and the major pity of my trials is that I have tended to ignore the magnificently rugged country we are travelling through.

I will have to come back and do this trip again – after I have done a moving-water kayak course.

kowhai colours a magical journey

Spring heralds its coming with a blaze of golden kowhai blossoms that even a damp Auckland cannot dim. And each year these yellow blooms bring a special treat for canoeists and those who prefer oar to outboard. For kowhai trees throw splashes of gold through the forest and urban garden alike, but most of all they seem to prefer to stare out over some body of water. It grows by river, lake, estuary or seashore, but perhaps the lordly kowhai is vain and hopes to catch a glimpse of its golden curls reflected in the water because it seems to save its best display for those quiet reaches where the water is indeed mirror calm.

When the kowhai trees, scraggly and near invisible all winter, suddenly shine in the bush canopy, it is time to check tide tables for a morning tide that will be full before wind or waterskiers ruffle it. There are many places the kowhai delivers its magic, but there can be none better than in the upper reaches of Lucas Creek in the upper Waitemata Harbour.

The creek runs nearly 7km from Rahui Beach at Greenhithe to Albany so to be there in time I must launch my kayak under the glow of a street light. There is a small boat ramp and – imbedded in a retaining wall and hidden by mangroves – a forgotten pile from the old Greenhithe wharf. A hundred years or so ago there might have been some workers waiting on the wharf in the darkness for a ferry to work or to send their fruit to the fledgling Auckland city markets.

These waterways were once major transport arteries for Maori and Pakeha settlers alike. Ngati Whatua and Te Kawerau a Maki paddled north past this beach to the Kaipara portage. In 1820 Samuel Marsden used the same route to go north, and a host of European settlers followed.

In the 1880s the s.s. *Gleaner* chugged past my launching spot on its way from Albany to Auckland. The service was so unreliable the residents of Lucas Creek formed a Steamboat Association, bought the little ship and renamed it the s.s. *Albany* to publicise the district. It sailed once a week in the fruit season to take strawberries and apples to Auckland, and once a fortnight out of season. Its steam donkey engine could be heard chug-chugging for miles, so upper harbour residents probably breathed a sigh of relief when the s.s. *Advance*, an 18-tonne ship built by Logan Brothers, took over the daily run to Riverhead.

All is quiet now as my kayak slips into the yacht-infested channel between Greenhithe and Herald Island. The island was named after Governor Hobson's ship, which ventured up here in 1840 in search of a site for a new capital. It is a good mooring spot because beneath the yachts is a river drowned when the last ice age melted about 12,000 years ago, and in the channel the water may be up to 18m deep.

Herald Island, once a favourite colonial picnic spot, was also a graveyard for old ships, but its significance for this voyage is that it shelters the 200m-wide entrance to Kaipatiki (the place where the flounder feeds), now called Lucas Creek after a flax miller. There is a deep hole at the entrance and the cantankerous water-flows on the ingoing and outgoing tides provide a textbook on estuary navigation. Choose the right 'lane' and you can easily paddle or sail against the tidal flow. In still water like this morning's the yachts swinging on their moorings will show even a novice the best route to take.

Past Salthouse's boatyard a stump of sandstone with a cable marker at its end is the eroded remains of the hole in the wall. A penniless young English lawyer, fresh off an immigrant ship, was found sheltering in this cave with his wife and small child. He survived to become Judge John Edwin MacDonald of the Native Lands Court.

Later an enterprising Lucas Creek settler, Thomas Hunter, used the cave to store petrol for his fleet of launches. Hunter began with one launch, the *Regal*, on which he and four of his seven sons travelled to the city to work each day. His next launch, the *Regal II*, bought in 1908, could make the journey from Greenhithe in just 30 minutes. Not surprisingly, others wanted to get a ride too. At its peak the Hunter's fleet carried 52,000 passengers a year from the upper harbour. They even had a special shallow-draught 56-passenger vessel for the tide-prone run to Albany.

The tide is nearly full as I pass Picnic Point, now an exclusive subdivision, and the wide mangrove-filled arm of the Te Wharau Creek. Across the channel on the Paremoremo shore is Whisky Cove. Until 1846 kauri forests lined both shores. Timbermen from the Bay of Islands and Whangaroa rafted the logs to the infant city for use in some of Auckland's earliest government buildings.

When they had done, gumdiggers moved in and burned what was left of the forest. It was a rough and smoky backwater, a haunt for runaway sailors, convicts, military deserters – and liquor smugglers. In one 1870 raid customs officers found two stills with a capacity of 100 gallons of whisky a day. The grog was smuggled into Auckland in cutters that sailed up to Lucas Creek to collect firewood.

The most important product to come out of Lucas Creek now, however, is distilled from its vast mangrove forests. They cover 45ha of the creek and each hectare produces 8 tonnes dry weight of detritus a year – four times more productive than the best pasture land and the most vital element in the marine food chain. Ahead of my kayak the still water is disturbed by the scurrying of tiny fish trying to escape yellow-eyed mullet as well as eagle-eyed kingfishers waiting in the mangrove branches.

Past Schnapper Rock Road, once the site of a huge gumdiggers' camp, the creek begins to narrow. On low spring tides most of the salt water will leave the creek above here, and after heavy rain the low-tide channel will be almost fresh, and muddy, with water running off the Albany Basin catchment.

Colemans Landing is now backed by the North Shore Golf Club. On the opposite shore a keen eye might spot some of the exotic trees that were planted around Creek House. The old house was long ago destroyed by fire but now, glowing on the steepening Paremoremo escarpment, are the kowhai blooms that have prompted this voyage.

In the narrowing creek, past Inghams Bend and near an old Albany wharf, almost the last port of call for the ferry launches, the water begins to look like the Ganges as the tubular kowhai flowers, nipped from their stalks and dropped by clumsy kereru (native pigeons), or blown by the wind, float lazily on the water. If nothing disturbed them the flowers might float back and forth for five days because that is how long it takes the water eventually to leave these upper reaches for the open harbour.

adventure log

GETTING THERE: Lucas Creek paddles usually begin at a boat ramp at the end of Rame Road, Greenhithe.

PADDLING TIME: Count on about 4 hours for the round trip – though you may do it in less. Depending on the timing of the tide, you could stop for a latte in Albany village.

MAP: LINZ R10.

FURTHER INFORMATION: The upper Waitemata Harbour has a fascinating history – found in libraries in self-published local histories on villages such as Greenhithe, Riverhead and Albany. A study of estuarine flora and fauna is also revealing.

Fortunately it is still today because, while the kowhai are beautiful, it is the nectaries hidden in their pendulous blossoms that give this canoe journey its magic. I stop paddling and listen to flocks of tui, as numerous as sparrows, flitting from one small pot of nectar to another. The birds are heard more than they are seen, the beating of wings like muffled timpani to their melodic song. In places the golden kowhai are splashed with shafts of clematis, as brilliant white as the tui throat ruff.

I am just a few paddle strokes from one of the fastest-developing regions in New Zealand, a splash away from a shopping centre, university and the main highway north. It is hard to believe until past the Oteha Stream – where the old Albany School is now an outdoor education centre that teaches hundreds of youngsters canoeing skills – when civilisation rears its ugly head with rubbish thrown over the bank.

Just past the remains of the Albany Landing and the graceful arch of Albany bridge is a delightful waterfall and reserve with a riverside walkway that is worth a 7km paddle to visit at any time of the year. But when the kowhai blooms on Lucas Creek it is a voyage to savour in the stillness of morning when there is little else about to disturb nature's magic.

From the summit of Rangitoto as the lights of the city come on and the sky slowly darkens, the great bulk of the Waitakere Ranges in the far distance stands almost black against the last tinges of natural light. In the crowd who have come to watch the day vanish from the best vantage point in the city someone wonders what is the cluster of red lights that appears buried in the Waitakere foothills.

And then it dawns on him. It is the Sky Tower reduced to relative insignificance. The volcanic island of Rangitoto, with its three-peak summit unchanging from any point on the compass, still lords it over any man-made viewing platform. That is possibly of some comfort to those standing on this natural basalt tower because they have gone to considerable effort to get there.

The landmark that no Aucklander can fail to recognise exploded out of the sea just 600 years ago. It is the youngest, largest and least weathered basalt volcano in New Zealand. It is also of international significance because of the way more than 200 species of native plants, dominated by pohutukawa forest, have colonised its 2333ha of barren lava.

If Rangitoto is Auckland's icon, an evening trip there by sea kayak to watch the sunset is a distinctly Auckland tradition that, under the watchful eye of competent guides, anyone of average fitness can do even if they have never been in a kayak.

We meet at St Heliers, where at this relatively late hour the Waitemata is still a busy harbour. There are fishers coming back at high speed from the Motuihe Channel, a keeler fleet racing back to Half Moon Bay and high-speed ferries toing and froing to Waiheke Island.

There is a north-easterly blowing and for half an hour or so we bend our backs into it. By sea-kayak cruising standards we are on a lazy pace, but then the fleet consists mostly of novice paddlers. As we move into the lee of Rangitoto the wind dies away and the seas flatten. It is dusk when we arrive at Rangitoto wharf and head up the easy trail to the volcano's summit.

This is a familiar journey for almost everyone in this group – but not at this time of the day. Instead of the sun bouncing its heat off the island's exposed black basalt, it is tinging the western sky over the city a pale gold. As we climb higher the colours are reflected in the harbour water while the downtown buildings and the harbour bridge blacken in profile.

By day the view of the harbour and Hauraki Gulf from this 280m vantage point is one of the grandest sights in the country and by night it is equally good. But the real joy of this particular adventure is in watching the evening tableau unfold. The lights pop on – or become evident – in a way that almost seems orchestrated. Tamaki Drive is lit, then the wharves, and so on.

We could probably sit here and meditate on our good fortune for hours but time and tide don't wait for such reflection. After the sights from the summit it might be imagined that the paddle back to St Heliers could be a bit of an anticlimax. Instead it is a magical way to conclude the adventure.

Kayaking in still night waters is a sensual experience. There is an unreal impression of speed that lifts tired spirits. The paddle blades and bow waves make sounds not noticeable in daylight. Small fish scurry away without warning. At one point there is a 'thunk' from my bow and a splash that suggests I have actually paddled into some fish lounging in the water.

Night paddling can be even more exciting when the water is thick with phosphorescence. Nonetheless, when we reach St Heliers the group is sated with pleasure. I am biased but I bet they feel a lot more enriched than most of the people who spent the evening at that other tower.

kayak purgatory

When a hardy settler generation calls a trail 'purgatory' it probably doesn't pay to ignore them. For hundreds of years Maori used what are now blue lines on a topographical map to travel from the Far North deep into Waikato without having to test their canoes in the rigours of the open sea. Where great harbours lay tantalisingly close, they hauled their canoes across the intervening land, sometimes leaving furrows in the ground that European settlers would later follow and dream of turning into canals.

The portages are famous in Maori lore but the Pakeha only gave one – the link between the Kaipara and Waitemata Harbours – the dubious title of the Portage. A modern map seems to show the logic of avoiding the treacherous Kaipara and Manukau bars when the Kaipara and Kumeu Rivers wind sinuously south to within a brief stroll of the Waitemata Harbour.

So down this route came war parties of Ngati Whatua from their southern Kaipara stronghold to lay tribal claim to the Auckland isthmus. They built a settlement at Pitoitoi (Brighams Creek) and another at Rangitopuni (Riverhead). From here in August 1820 Samuel Marsden with his Ngapuhi guide Te Morenga travelled to the Kaipara and on to the Bay of Islands.

Not many people have willingly faced the tortuous, mostly swampy, 23km Kaipara portage to Helensville since – which makes it a tempting adventure. Incurable enthusiast Joe Scott-Woods and kayaking guru Peter Sommerhalder agree to join me on the Portage.

While most of the city still sleeps we slip our kayaks into the water at Greenhithe and paddle on to an incoming tide to Riverhead. We have the still water to ourselves and reach our haul-out spot within an hour. Our kayaks are strapped on to trolleys and, to the accompaniment of a couple of barking dogs and the bemused gaze of a woman still in her nightie, we trundle off up Kaipara Portage Road towards Kumeu.

When we reach Kumeu and the Highway 16 bridge across the Kumeu River, we have strolled less than 5km in an hour with less effort than pulling a golf trundler, and this is Kumeu, the place where, it is said, hauling stops. The trickle of water under the bridge is hardly suitable for a sea kayak but floating a canoe should be easier than hauling it.

They thought so last century because further up-river the headwaters are only a stone's throw from Brighams Creek. In 1865 it was proposed that a canal should be built between the two. By then anything was considered to be better than facing the purgatory of the Portage. A route for war parties and missionaries might be one thing; moving the goods and produce of European settlers by bullock dray across the swampy valley was another.

When the settlers bound for Albertland in 1862 were forced to reach the Kaipara by the Portage, most vowed never to face the journey again, preferring to sail around North Cape into the harbour. There were 30 to 40 bridges along the route and because of flooding they were always in need of repair. In the winter the Portage to Helensville was mostly an impassable quagmire. Relief came with the first train from Riverhead to Helensville in 1875.

We intend to conquer this route and so far it is hard to see what all the fuss was about last century. The river, which is really a creek, is choked with weeds so high that often all we can see of each other is a raised paddle blade. In other places oxygen weed is so thick that our kayaks grind to a halt. But it is still a lot of fun to paddle along this weed-infested creek, and when we reach a major road bridge in an hour our spirits are high and we tuck in to a mid-morning snack. From here it's downhill all the way to Helensville on what should be an ever-widening river.

Onwards we paddle with wonderful confidence. A hot swim at Parakai beckons. Beautiful red dragonflies hover all around us. Privet and manuka drop their blossoms on the water and ducks squawk and splash from under overhanging branches.

About midday I am beginning to think something is not quite right. The river has less water than when we began and the banks are thickly wooded, whereas by my estimation the land should be opening out into swampy toetoe flats. Worst of all are the trees that have fallen off the bank to block the river. Oxygen weed and watercress have become wistful memories as we haul our relatively heavy 5m kayaks across log-jam after log-jam. At times when I get out of my stranded kayak I sink to my waist in foul-smelling mud.

Rusted 44-gallon drums, old fence posts, concrete debris and bits of discarded clothing are stuck high in a tree where the last flood deposited them. The river bank is several metres above us. We could be up some filthy river in the Amazonian jungle if it wasn't for the man-made debris. What lies beneath the muddy, log-strewn waters and under the banks doesn't bear thinking about. So we don't, until Scott-Woods finds a small buoy and hauls an eel net out to show us its bounty of two eels, each more than 1m long and thicker than your arm.

The river winds around itself like the eels in the net and bears no resemblance to the spot on the map where I think we are. I am dispirited but fortunate to have happy companions. Something is wrong. We stop for a late lunch beside a delightful grove of stately totara, straight, canoe-making specimens. It is a measure of the perverse river that from our lunch spot we haul our kayaks 30m across a paddock and save about 200m of river travel and 20 log-jams.

The afternoon becomes a succession of short paddles, man-hauling, cursing, floundering, ducking under trees or crawling over them. It's an adventure, says Scott-Woods. At last we reach a house, a telephone and then a road bridge. When I clamber up to it, nearly 7 hours after we entered the water, I find with disbelief that it is the Waimauku bridge, just 6.5km in a straight line from where we started paddling.

I am tired, sore and badly scratched. The Portage has sent another victim to purgatory and we are less than halfway there. It's time to go home.

adventure log

GETTING THERE: Only the slightly demented would want to make this trip but a reasonable flat water journey on the Kaipara River would start at the end of Wharepapa Road, off SH 16 to Helensville.

PADDLING TIME: 3 to 4 hours for the bottom half of the river.

MAP: LINZ Q10.

BE INSPIRED: There is no shortage of weed-infested creeks on which to go exploring in a small plastic kayak. Better still if it is to repeat some historic journey.

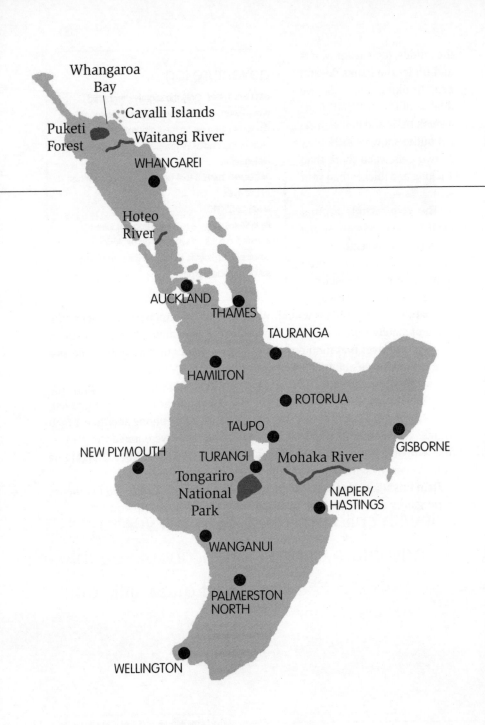

you're never too young

Bilbo Baggins should have asked children before declaring, 'Adventures…nasty, disturbing, uncomfortable things! Make you late for dinner. I can't see what anyone sees in them.' There is nothing, absolutely nothing, in the outdoors better than sharing it with children. They will open your eyes to adventure, magic, indescribable beauty – and just a few little epics.

fly by night

Adventure travel is an effortless indulgence for children. Adults may scour route guides to away-from-it-all outdoor locations or dream of treks to exotic places overseas but for children an outdoor adventure may be as close as the back lawn.

That was where we pitched a cotton canvas pup tent, more decades ago than I care to admit. It was stamped 'Le Roy' and proofed with a sticky concoction that gave the interior a fragrance that was unmistakably of outdoor adventure. Any old piece of canvas made a groundsheet and the earliest of airbeds our mattress. The most comfortable volume of air was forever elusive but we were snug in a crude sleeping bag, home-made from old blankets. A small fruit box held the essential paraphernalia of all intrepid explorers and a candle on a baking-powder tin lid. The wooden tent poles had a few small nails hammered into them on which we hung our sheath knife, compass and hat.

There, in the deepest, darkest reaches of the back lawn we spent many summer evenings – unless of course, it rained (or the hedgehogs snuffled too disconcertingly). Our parents snuck down with torches to check on us, only we didn't know until years later.

Some things never change. At the beach in summer my children sleep on stretchers in one of those modern frame tents that are light years from the creations of 'Le Roy'. It is no place for young adventurers, so a pup tent donated by some departing overseas travellers is nagged into service. 'Le Roy' would have cringed at the Korean workmanship; the kids are ecstatic. Real adventure is to be had inside a flimsy bit of nylon just a few metres from the opulent canvas structure now dubbed the 'dog' tent.

But in the pecking order of adventure something even better is to come. We pack up our sleeping bags and a pup tent fly, and with a farmer's permission head over the hills to a deserted bay. When you are just five and six years old a sleeping bag and a raincoat is a handsome load to fit into a school rucksack. And a 'tent' with neither a floor nor ends to it is high adventure indeed.

A plastic survival tube is rigged at one end to deflect the breeze. The young adventurers decline to hunker down behind it. Their bellies satisfied by barbecued sausages, baked potatoes and toasted marshmallows, they nod off, gazing out the open end towards the sea, the dying campfire and the tables and chairs they have fashioned from driftwood logs.

adventure log

GETTING THERE: Anywhere from a back lawn to a deserted scrap of coast.

CAMPING TIME: Overnight so you can watch the sun go down and come up.

BE INSPIRED: No Kiwi should need a manual for an expedition like this. All you need is imagination and parenting skills. A background in Scouting and children who have learned self-reliance and imagination through the Playcentre movement, may help too.

In the morning they lift the side of the fly and announce, quite unconcerned, that some curious cattle are close by. You can't spot that from a stretcher in a dog tent. They swim, cook breakfast over a fire, make a fort from driftwood and catch a small fish each off the rocks that enclose the bay. But the draughty fly tent is the real adventure.

'Can we sleep in the fly tent again?' they plead when our mini-trek is over. About the same time, a neighbouring adult complains about being too old for camping. Creature comforts, not canvas, are more alluring.

Try telling that to the kids. Better still, try to imagine what it is that attracts them – and probably once you – to sleeping out under a primitive fabric shelter. What innocence turns a shell into a vase and fills it with dandelions to grace a driftwood log table? Or finds excitement in observing the tiny creatures left behind in rock pools – and contentment under a simple fly tent?

Somewhere out there in the darkness there is another world. Such are the things a parent contemplates in a fly tent pitched on a deserted foreshore while his children sleep soundly, dreaming dreams of youthful adventure.

running down the waitangi

The Waitangi River rises high on an escarpment beyond the Bay of Islands. Just a few kilometres further west is the Puketi State Forest and a catchment system that delivers its water to the Hokianga Harbour and the Tasman Sea. But the Waitangi carries its weeping waters east along one of the most historic routes in the country.

Near the headwaters of the Waitangi is Lake Omapere and the site of a bloody battle in May 1845 between the warriors of Hone Heke and British troops. A little down-river is Waimate North and the mission house established in 1832. Not far away is the oldest oak tree in New Zealand, planted in 1824, and the site of the first flour mill.

Historic pa sites abound along the broad valley down which the Waitangi carves a convoluted path. This is no mighty Waikato transporting vast volumes of water, a turbulently tumbling Tongariro draining snowy peaks, or an inland highway like the Whanganui. It is frustratingly narrow and shallow and perversely turning this way and that. Somewhere along its path came Maori warriors and missionaries but they surely used the Waitangi as route-finder more than a route.

The first obstruction the river presents to navigation tends to be insurmountable. Sea kayakers paddle past the Waitangi National Reserve and up the mangrove-lined Waitangi River estuary. Suddenly a basalt rock ledge rises to block their way, and that of any salt water too. It is a mark of the trip to place the kayak bow under the water curtain of the Haruru Falls but the kayakers can go no further.

What lies above the falls need not be mystery. Graham Egarr noted in his canoeing guide to North Island rivers that the Waitangi can be run under most flow conditions, with rock ledges creating runnable falls – including the Haruru – and with rapids higher in the river that do not exceed grade two.

It is a tempting diversion from sand and surf so on a day when onshore winds tend to rule out the sea, we load a small kayak and a cheap plastic inflatable into the car and drive to Puketona Junction, where the road to Paihia leaves Highway 10. Our mission is to run the Waitangi as far as the falls. What we will find and how long our journey will take is unknown.

The Highway 10 bridge nearest the junction is actually across the Waiaruhe River, which joins the Waitangi a few hundred metres further on. With safe parking nearby it is a logical place to put in. We clamber down a steep bank to the river and pump up our inflatable on a broad rock ledge beneath the bridge.

There is not a lot of water in the river, nor is there much flow. The inflatable, which is not much more than a toy, seems to prefer to go in all directions except straight ahead. But when the day is relatively young and paddlers are fresh and excited who cares about eccentric navigation?

Inflatable and kayak drift lazily down the narrow and mostly overgrown stream. Where thick carpets of weed, sand bars or debris block our way, it is necessary to get out and do a little pushing. The children in the inflatable don't mind one bit. Judging by the giggling that accompanies these wading excursions, it's as much fun as playing in the surf, especially if you fall overboard, accidentally on purpose, of course. A couple of small rapids are even more fun, although it can be a bit hard on the knees in a craft not designed for river running.

It is perhaps as well that we are having fun on the water because the river would hardly rate for its scenery. It has mostly cut deep into the valley so that the banks are often high above us. We can see it is generally farmland. There are a few tall trees on the side of the river but no native bush canopy.

But there are other compensations. We reach a long, broad pool flanked on one side by a sandy beach. Attached to a tree at one end of the pool and rising to a cliff at the other end is a flying fox. I paddle to the centre of the pool and retrieve the rope that is attached to the flying fox 'carriage'. The children, who have beached their inflatable and swum to the base of the cliff, take the rope and climb as high as their courage will take them. Then, with an appropriate yell, they launch themselves into space, dropping into the river.

The basalt rock ledges Egarr warned us of are another compensation. In places they throw up barriers that cannot be navigated with the low summer flow and we must portage kayak and raft down the rock until we reach clear water again. But in other sections the water bubbles over the rocks in sufficient quantity for us to follow. Often the rock cuts the river into narrow chutes down which we drop like the flying fox.

At one place a narrow chute to the left carries a good quantity of fast water while that to the right is wide, shallow and tame. Between them is an island of willow trees. Stay here until I have checked it out, I caution the crew of the inflatable as I nose into the fast water on the left.

Long before I am out of earshot I am yelling 'not this way' because ahead of me is a willow branch right across the chute at about waist height. I am trapped on a watery roller-coaster. I cannot stop or turn. I clutch at the branch while my kayak carries on alone, careering down the river before rolling over and disappearing into the island of willows.

My predicament would be hysterical to followers of slapstick. Eventually I loosen grip, slide under branch and follow kayak down the chute. It takes a considerable effort against the current to drag my waterlogged craft from under the willows and onto the bank so I can empty it. Then I walk upstream to guide my companions down the safe route. Fortunately no harm is done apart from one drowned camera.

Now the flow seems to lessen and grow more lazy. The children, trying valiantly to paddle an ungainly craft, wilt with it. A tow rope to my kayak keeps us moving. The book promises that we will take out at the Lily Pond, below a small waterfall. But where is it? We have been at it for over 4 hours and a flagging paddler suggests I have a habit of underestimating the time it takes for our adventures.

As the river winds around and around the inflatable is proving quite frustrating and useless in these low flow conditions. Eventually I see a house and trek through a paddock to seek some reassurance. It's not far, I'm told, so with spirits somewhat more buoyant we paddle on.

After 5 hours on the river we reach the promised waterfall, which seems a bit more substantial than Egarr suggests, and then a huge swimming hole that can only be the Lily Pond.

There are footprints in the sand, beer cans and wheel tracks. We are back in civilisation.

Joy is a deserted bay, Mum cooking sausages and baked potatoes on an open fire, and a night camped under a fly sheet.

Mt Ngauruhoe may well be Mt Everest for a couple of young hikers clambering up the Mangatepopo valley on the Tongariro Northern Circuit.

An overnight snow storm brings an early winter to the Round the Mountain Track near Mangaehuehu Hut, Mt Ruapehu.

Dad gives a helping hand to a young battler on the Round the Mountain Track, Mt Ruapehu.

Another little epic: all the better for the young battler to remember a mountain journey with my Dad.

When at last the sun comes out so do the smiles and high jinks on the circuit around Mt Ruapehu.

Wading the Waipapa River in the Puketi Forest, Northand, is great fun – for a while.

a room with a view

A room with arguably the best view in the central North Island costs just $8 a night. From a warm and comfortable bunk in Ketetahi Hut you can stare down the Pacific ring of fire and watch the golden orb of the sun rise somewhere off East Cape. While you cannot see as far as Tonga, at the other end of a line of volcanoes that stretches from Mt Ruapehu, or even White Island, you can see the brooding bulk of Mt Tarawera back-lit on the skyline. Steam from the Wairakei thermal area rises ghost-like in front of it.

If a five-year-old daughter is snuggled beside you she will likely gasp at the brilliance of the sun as it glints on the vastness of Lake Taupo – and excitedly wake her slumbering seven-year-old brother to share the experience.

Just 1800 years ago this very area exploded in one of the most massive eruptions the world has seen. Up to 100km³ of red-hot pumice spewed out over an area from Hamilton in the north to Palmerston North in the south. This morning the lake that fills the caldera left behind by the volcano is serene: early-morning fishermen can be imagined, if not exactly visible.

The long-extinct Pihanga – much more lovely from the south – still shades Lake Rotoaira, where fishing boats can be seen making long, thin incisions on a mirror surface. Mt Tongariro, on which lies our 1430m-high vantage point, is quiet too. Once it angrily sent Mt Taranaki into exile for daring to covet the love of the beautiful forest-clad Pihanga – as a daughter familiar with the Maori legend reminds me.

Yet in 1896 the nearby upper Te Mari crater sent ash as far away as Napier and a broad swathe of mosses and small shrubs is unable to hide the 800-years-young river of lava that flowed down from Te Mari into the bush we tramp through to reach Ketetahi.

It has taken us a leisurely four-and-a-bit hours, lunch included, to trek from the car park on Highway 47 through the Hall's totara forest of Okahukura Bush to the hut. With each child carrying a rucksack with their sleeping bag and warm clothes, and Dad everything else, we set off in a noisy excitement

adventure log

GETTING THERE: The track to Ketetahi Hut starts off Highway 46 near Turangi. It is advisable to use a shuttle service rather than leave your car.
WALKING TIME: It takes about 3½ hours to walk to Ketetahi Hut.
MAP: Tongariro Parkmap 273-04.
FURTHER INFORMATION: Consult TONGARIRO AND TAUPO WALKS by Alan Williamson. The track is well marked and formed. DOC Turangi 0-7-386 8607 will give weather information and sell hut tickets. The hut will be crowded in peak season.

that drowns out the bird life. The Ketetahi springs, their rising steam visible to motorists crossing the Pihanga saddle, were known to Maori for their health-giving properties, and lie in a tiny enclave of Ngati Tuwharetoa land. Tourists have travelled to the healing waters for more than 100 years, at first by riverboat to Pipiriki and stagecoach to a hut near the steaming, sulphurous springs. Today Ngati Tuwharetoa ask those who pass by the springs to not bathe there.

The track steepens as it nears the bushline, with giant-sized steps that are a major effort for tiny legs. A walking stick collected on the way helps. But above the lookout and the first view of Lake Rotoaira, and the sudden change to alpine tussock shrubland, the slope is steady rather than steep. Several large snow patches cross our path to add to the adventure.

There is more at the hut: a Boys Brigade party from Hamilton, several young trampers, including some from overseas, and an older couple whom we share a room with. You cannot book a bed in the 24-bunk Ketetahi Hut. No matter; mountain huts are naked without people. There is always somewhere to sleep, even if it is under the table. It is the camaraderie that blossoms within them that causes huts, rusty corrugated-iron hovels and all, to be given almost human qualities by those who carve their names into roof beams.

The children rest their tired muscles in front of the fire, their eyes darting at the human activity, and soon make friends with those who share their mountain shelter. The thermal area was exciting but it is the hut the children came for. They eat by candlelight and share tramping tales with the older children like mountain veterans. Dinner eaten and water for the next day filtered – signs warning of giardia and possum droppings on the water tanks suggest there is no safety in rain water – sleep comes quickly.

Next year we might stay and climb the mountain. The children want to spend the night in a snow cave somewhere.

a ramble in paradise

Some of the best trips into the hills are long in gestation, and a two-day tramp that has been kicking around in a rucksack map pocket for a couple of years is an adventure that deserves the huge high-pressure weather system that smiles on it.

Since we kicked off a ski holiday with an overnighter in Ketetahi Hut, on the flanks of Mt Tongariro, there has been a promise to stay in a mountain hut again. But the promise remains unfulfilled because whenever the weather is too bad to go skiing it is also too dangerous to go walking into alpine regions. And if Hughie the weather god is smiling, ski boots seem to take precedence over tramping boots.

In summer the mountains of Tongariro National Park ring to the boots of walkers and climbers with no such temptations. Easter may now have gone but there still seems time for us to be counted among the summer ramblers before the winter snows set in.

Thieves have done Tongariro hikers a service of sorts; with just one car and driver the trip we plan would never have been possible without a shuttle service to avert the devastation suffered when returning to a burgled car. At the end of Mangatepopo Road we consign our car to the care of Clark Eivin, shoulder our packs and turn towards Mt Ngauruhoe, already sporting a bewitching topping of snow.

This is the start point of the Tongariro Crossing, the all-day walk that is invariably dubbed the best one-day walk in the country. It is also one of the entry-exit points for the Tongariro Northern Circuit, one of New Zealand's Great Walks. A friend through here recently on a Saturday shared the track with about 200 others. At the Mangatepopo Hut the warden says hundreds of secondary-school students have crossed almost daily on school trips this year.

They must be doing classroom work for we have the valley, brilliant sunshine and cloudless universe to ourselves. It is a lot better than school, at least until we begin to climb the steep lava flows to the Mangatepopo Saddle.

The reward at the top is a clear view across to the perfect cone of Mt Taranaki and patches of snow that invite a snowball battle between mouthfuls of lunch. If there is a perfect time of year to be in alpine regions, this seems to be it.

Others must think so too. Across the flat, volcanic ash expanse of South Crater – which is not really a crater at all but a drainage basin – we are passed by three young German tourists equipped for a stroll around the city markets. Today they will make it easily; sometime this year one of their countrymen probably won't.

Red Crater at 1886m above sea level is the highest point of the crossing and our trek. To our left is a poled route to the Tongariro summit, to our right the livid, steaming scar of the crater, a steep and frightening entry into the bowels of the earth that my young companions understandably decide is best not to get too close to.

Across the abyss lies our destination, the Oturere valley, but we skirt around the crater rim and down a loose ash and scoria ridge to the Emerald Lakes. Fed by minerals washed from Red Crater, they are three brilliant jewels on the edge of the vast Central Crater. In the distance is the equally jewel-like Blue Lake.

The track to Ketetahi heads north across this crater like a slug trail in the desert. We turn east between the Emerald Lakes and head down the Oturere valley, just as did lava that flowed from Red Crater. When the molten rock cooled it left a jagged rock garden, rising in clumps from a springy mix of scoria and ash.

We have been on the trail for 7½ hours – including some generous breaks – when we reach Oturere Hut, our refuge for the night. Oturere is one of the newer huts. It is also the least used – which is one reason we chose the route. As it transpires, our fears are groundless. The busy time on this increasingly popular trek ends around Easter. We have the luxury of Oturere's 24 bunks and thick mattresses to ourselves.

Space for a couple of young companions exuberant at having completed a long mountain crossing is not the only luxury. This is a Great Walk hut and there are gas cookers and push-button gas heaters. Although there is not a tree in nearly 2 hours' walk, according to the visitors' book an 'aggressive possum' has kept Mike Birch of the United States and Jorg Sigel from Germany 'at bay till late in the night'. The hut warden has noticed the entry and by 7pm when I step out to admire the crisp, clear evening and Ngauruhoe and Ruapehu revealed in the moonlight, the marauding marsupial has made a fatal move into a trap.

You sleep well in the silence of a warm and empty mountain hut after a long day's tramp. And you gasp with pure pleasure when the sun rises above the Kaimanawa Range and blasts through the hut door on another perfect day. The air at 1350m is so clear it seems to cleanse with every breath. That must be why we set off for Waihohonu almost lightheaded, across the loose gravel foothills of Ngauruhoe and up and down a number of dry stream valleys.

adventure log

GETTING THERE: A trek on the Tongariro Northern Circuit generally begins at the end of the Mangatepopo Road, off Highway 47 between Turangi and National Park.

WALKING TIME: The northern circuit takes at least three days but you can shortern it to two by leaving at Waihohonu on the Desert Road.

MAP: Tongariro Parkmap 273-04.

FURTHER INFORMATION: This is potentially dangerous alpine country and you should consult DOC Whakapapa 0-7-892 3729 for track and weather conditions. See also NEW ZEALAND'S GREAT WALKS by Pearl Hewson.

Eventually a beech forest that has escaped the ravages of volcanic eruption softens our path. The forest shade is welcome because the track climbs a ridge at a grade that is not quite so funny. Down the other side is the new Waihohonu Hut and its flush toilets. Across the stream that feeds their cisterns is the old hut, its sturdy corrugated-iron walls newly painted post office red.

It's worth a small detour to show a couple of young companions who have just spent the night in gas-fired luxury the sort of bunks trampers of old slept in. The historic hut was built in 1901 by the Department of Tourist and Health Resorts to provide the first accommodation for tourists in the national park. Visitors came to 'Mountain House' by coach or buggy on a small detour from the Desert Road, built between Waiouru and Tokaanu just a few years earlier. For 20 years the old Waihohonu Hut was the centre of activities in the park.

William Mead and Bernard Drake came here in 1913 with their recently imported skis and in deep snow on Tama Ridge behind the hut became the first to use skis on Mt Ruapehu. When their winter holiday was over a new era for the park had begun. From their exploring they concluded the Whakapapa slopes were better for skiing, and they organised a ski club.

On our 90-minute walk down the old buggy track to the Desert Road and Eivin waiting with our car, my companions conclude that the old-timers knew what luxury was. They rode in the comfort of a horse-drawn buggy from the road right to the hut door.

back-country notes

Huts in the back country have long contained a record of those who shelter in them. On tables and benches are scrawled, and often carved, the names of generations of trampers, climbers, hunters and shepherds. Some have wearily lain in top bunks and doodled on the rafter beams as they sheltered while a storm raged outside. Anywhere else and their efforts would be considered vandalism. But in old back-country huts the graffiti is more like a tableau of the history of outdoor recreation.

The construction of modern huts tends to deter such defacing: taking a pocket knife to a laminated beam smacks too much of anti-social behaviour. Fortunately the visitors' book is an alternative canvas on which to record a potted history of the hut and those who venture in.

In DOC huts the standard book asks visitors to 'leave details of planned route. This information will help us assist you if you become lost or injured.' Those who write they are going to the planet of the apes will obviously have no trouble assimilating when they get there. The department bravely remarks, 'We are also interested in your opinion of DOC facilities and service.' It is an invitation, it seems, that few of the thousands who traverse the volcanic craters and glacial valleys of this World Heritage area can resist.

Many are overseas tourists and, increasingly, many are New Zealand students compelled by their schools into adventure in the country's first national park. In good weather the northern circuit can be completed in about three days but in this deceptively fascinating country a more leisurely, explorer's pace is preferable.

It is easy to misjudge the Tongariro National Park until you set foot among its mysteries. It is of such geological wonder that the apparent sameness of the terrain is merely an illusion that disappears the closer you get. One valley is clearly the site of an ancient glacier, with the track winding up and down the moraines. Another may have a flow of lava down it and thick layers of ash exposed by wind and rain.

So my children and I continue on the Northern Circuit at an inquisitive pace. Last year we tramped up the Mangatepopo valley and crossed to the Desert Road in two days. This year we begin at the Whakapapa visitors' centre.

The Taranaki Falls is a pleasant spot for lunch and to indulge in the experience of walking under a waterfall without getting wet. The wide, metalled tourist track finishes here but the route past Tama Lakes to Waihohonu is well marked and well trodden.

Across this saddle between Mt Ngauruhoe and Mt Ruapehu came some of the first to seek recreation in these hills. They travelled from the old hut at Waihohonu towards Whakapapa in search of ski slopes. We tramp the other way and the only snow is an old remnant high on Mt Ruapehu that, as my young daughter observes, has melted into the outline of a face just beneath Te Heuheu.

In the gathering dusk the white face on the mountain grows ever more distinct. It is almost dark when we spot a tiny pinpoint of light in the beech forest that signals we will soon reach the shelter and warmth of the new Waihohonu hut. There is no one home but the hut warden, Thomas, who quickly lights some more candles and turns the gas heater on to welcome us.

This is luxury and there are flush toilets too. What would the old-timers whose names are carved into the old hut think of this? 'Thank God for flushable loos,' noted a recent visitor from Waikato Dio whose group's main activity was recorded as 'more bitching'. They can forgive foreigners who snore and smelly, fly-populated loos, but three days without a shower – and no guys – was a bit much.

It may be as well the girls were not sharing the hut in April with Damien Patterson and Tim Storey from Britain. They left the next day on the run from pensioners, snoring and the over-seventies' serious bridge club. Ten days later Emma Cooper complained it was very smelly and there were too many Australians. Kristel Blit from Belgium reckoned the $12 a night hut fee was too expensive but pity more her poor countryman, De Roo Niek. He miserably noted that he was drowning in teenagers, and so he was. There were nine from Hamilton Dio facing unhygienic toilets, ugly guys and no telephone, 24 from Fraser High, who said the trip was too long and the packs too heavy, and there was nowhere to sleep, another 24 from Hamilton dreaming of McDonald's in Taupo, and Emma Weston who couldn't wait to get home to television.

It could be depressing if the Carmine family from Waihi had not found 'rad' toilets, good weather, lovely scenery and, in the handwriting of someone much younger than De Roo Niek's nightmare hutmates, 'a cool clown face on the mountain'. It is still there as we stare out the hut door in the wan moonlight.

We have to agree with Rob Marshall of Turangi who recorded it's a great place to be. Well done, DOC, the facilities are worth an extra $4, wrote a group from Whangarei. I wonder if they were also brought a morning coffee while they lay in their sleeping bag?

Breakfast done, we leave our packs and take a short walk to the Ohinepango Springs, which are remarkable for the volume of water that gushes from beneath an old lava flow. On a warmer day the clear water would be irresistible. Instead we collect our packs and head north across a landscape that Lilach Ganon from Israel, like countless other tourists, suggested is like walking across the moon.

This is familiar country but the series of erosion gullies past the Waihohonu Stream still try to trick us. Is the ridge on the far side the last we have to climb or is it just another 'trickytop'? Trickytops becomes a game that even with a change in the weather and the beginning of light drizzle is much better than whingeing about 'sore feet, sore shoulders and awful weather' as did another Waikato Dio sixth-form group.

When we reach Oturere Hut it is empty of the 23 females and one male – 'Don't you wish you were here?' – who shared the hut on another occasion. We have the spacious hut to ourselves. As the wind rises outside, we sit in front of the cosy heater and play cards and read stories by flickering candlelight.

We have a particular affection for isolated Oturere. As Babs Fairchild of Adelaide noted, it has – weather permitting – fantastic views and all mod cons. The 'cons' included long-drop toilets. The problem, the visitors' book repeatedly reveals, was flies and, as Macchteld Baijet of Amsterdam complained, the 'bad air'. 'We refuse to use the thing they call a long-drop.' It prompted the rejoinder from the next visitor: don't go walking if you can't handle it. (The long-drops have since been replaced by sealed vault toilets, partly because people like the sensitive Dutch visitor chose to foul surrounding rocky outcrops and tussock clumps.)

Last summer there was even more to complain of, because there was no loo paper and from Perth to New York they grizzled about not being warned. 'Why don't you bring your own, you lazy people, this is not the Sheraton,' commented John Deringer of Melbourne.

We have toilet paper – our own as well as that provided by DOC – no flies and no smell. Unfortunately we don't have the 'sun, sun, sun' that greeted Mario Puccio of Palermo. It is raining and blowing strongly as we head up the

Oturere valley towards the Emerald Lakes and central crater. The wind chill is high but we are well protected against the hypothermia that strikes too many tourists on this route. In a couple of hours we are protected too by the lee of Mt Tongariro as the front swings west as predicted.

Deserted Ketetahi Hut – 'I'm off to the hot pools' was the last entry in the visitors'

adventure log

GETTING THERE: Start at the Whakapapa Visitor Centre, near the Chateau on SH 48, and travel via Waihohonu to exit through Ketetahi.

WALKING TIME: Three days.

MAP: Tongariro Parkmap 273-04.

FURTHER INFORMATION: For a different perspective on the Northern Circuit read DOC's THE RESTLESS LAND: THE STORY OF TONGARIRO NATIONAL PARK and TONGARIRO: A SACRED GIFT by Craig Potton. Also NORTH ISLAND BACKCOUNTRY HUTS by Hans Willems.

book – is a warm spot to lunch and dry out. Now it's only a couple of hours to the road-end where there is an information centre. If there was a visitors' book there too we would have written 'Northern Circuit complete, great walk, great kids, off for a hot soak at Tokaanu and to start the Southern Circuit – next year.'

Being lost in the Rangipo Desert in 9pm darkness and a rising wind is frightening when you are just 10 years old and tired after a long day's tramping.

'Dad, why do our trips always turn into epics?' my daughter asks accusingly.

'It's more fun,' I reply, not too convincingly because, brave though she is being, I am starting to get a little worried.

We are safe enough with sleeping bags, bivvy sacks, warm clothing, boulders the size of houses to shelter behind – and a cellphone – but this is no way to resume our three-year circumnavigation of Tongariro National Park. We have covered the entire northern circuit in a series of previous May tramps and now it is time to head south on the Round-the-Mountain track. The long-range forecast is fair, not bad enough for us to cancel our plans.

It is around 11.30am before we leave the Desert Road at the start of the track to Waihohonu and 2pm when we pack away our lunch and leave the Ohinepango Springs for the Rangipo Hut. There is a 5-hour tramp across the moonscape of the Rangipo Desert in front of us but it is not difficult terrain and we are on time when we reach the Tukino access road at 5pm and a sign tells us we have 2 hours to go.

But the pace slows appreciably; a sore ankle has become so painful that my daughter whimpers with each step. One nasty tumble that grazes her nose and badly bruises a knee knocks what is left of her confidence and spirit. Darkness falls before we reach the Whangaehu River but it is not yet an epic; it is a clear night and Joe and my son will have the billy on when we arrive.

All afternoon we have followed the route poles. Now my torch picks out the reflective square nailed to their tops. The Whangaehu has been a worry all day because we know that the lahar that spewed out of the crater of Mt Ruapehu last year knocked out the footbridge across it. What we don't know is that the mudslide, many metres deep, has also knocked out crucial route poles.

It is salutary to remember that on Christmas Eve 1953 a wall in the crater lake of Ruapehu breached and a flood wave travelling at 900m³/s surged down this same river. The wall of water, sand, silt and boulders knocked away the rail bridge at Tangiwai, 30km away, just minutes before the Auckland express train arrived. One hundred and fifty-one people were killed.

Now, in the moonlight, the river is a seething sheet of white and beyond it are high bluffs. Where do we cross? There is no sign of any poles but I find a small stone cairn and I have a reasonable fix on where I last saw Joe shine his torch. When we get to the water's edge I know why he hasn't waited. The water is only ankle-deep and underfoot is sand.

The eastern and southern flanks of Mt Ruapehu are an endless series of ravines scoured out by rivers and glaciers. We find an easy route over the bluff but the route poles remain elusive. My torch cannot pick them out because reflectors are nailed only to the side facing the track.

After breasting a couple more gullies we shelter among the rocks on a ridge top. We could be above or below the track, and thus the hut, and it is difficult to tell from the topographical map just how many gullies we should cross. It is time, while my brave young companion still has a stiff upper lip and is warm, to stop, get into our sleeping bags and wait for daylight, or for Joe to return.

When the wind veers slightly we move to the other side of the ridge and as I cast my torch around in the distance I get the vague idea of seeing something that could be a pole, or it could be pumice? I clamber off the ridge of rock down into an ash-covered gully to investigate, and with immense relief find a line of poles about 100m up the mountain.

It is after 9pm and there is not a lot you can do to make things better except to give your daughter a kiss and tell her you love her. There are several more gullies to traverse but we meet Joe, who has come back to look for us. When we reach the hut and its fire at 10.30pm the misery of the last few hours evaporates.

It could have been worse. For possibly 500,000 years this desolate land-scape has been modified by volcanic explosion as the Indian-Australian tectonic plate collides with the Pacific plate 60km off the east coast and the disturbed magma seeks a weakness in the Earth's crust. In AD181 the molten brew exploded out of Lake Taupo, sending a column of angry pumice more than 50km into the sky. Lava flowed through the area at more than 600km/h. In China a court historian, Hou Han Shui, recorded that all the horizon was as red as blood. A Roman historian recorded the heavens were ablaze.

The forests to the east of Mt Ruapehu were reduced to charred remnants that Maori folklore warns against using to make charcoal fires lest a spirit chief sends a sudden deathly storm. With its forest mantle burnt and buried beneath a layer of ash and pumice, Rangipo was destined to become a haunted, gale-swept desert of soft dunes where boots leave the imprint of a moon-walker.

The missionary explorer William Colenso described the desert as a fit place for Macbeth's witches but in the morning the scene we wake to is sunshine, happy faces and, while the wind is gathering force, clear skies. We face a 5- to 6-hour trek at adult speed to the Mangaehuehu Hut at 1300m on the southern slopes of Ruapehu. A book describes the route as a 'gradual descending sidle' but it takes no account of a sore ankle and the wind gusts that knock my daughter to her knees.

Rain squalls come horizontally. The steepness of old glacial moraine and the sharp drop into many stream-beds take their toll on young morale. The wind chill is bitter and I am worried; this area is too exposed for my liking. So after a damp lunch Joe goes on to the hut where there will be three men who passed us earlier. My son takes over the navigation and keeps his sister moving. I have her pack on my chest and can't see much at all. We are sidling down but we are far from out – but it is hard to get much response to my jokes.

Spirits rise when we reach the shelter of mountain beech trees but there is still a long plod to go. Half an hour from the hut Joe and two of the other group arrive. A warm fire and hot chocolate again evaporate the misery of a $7^1/_2$-hour tramp into a gale. Is there anything more resilient than children?

Denis, Noel and Graham are from Wanganui and have been tramping together for 15 years. Their company is good for us. The met forecast on my cellphone promises snow to 900m.

During the night the wind howls around the chimney. In the morning it is quiet. But outside, excited children tell me, there is at least 15cm of snow that closes the Desert Road and blankets Ohakune.

They can probably hear our groans from there as we gingerly push our feet into freezing, wet boots. Our three hut companions leave before us and we follow the trail they have beaten. Toes soon warm in woollen socks and so does our mood. The wind has gone, and blue sky and sun appear.

Duckboards have been constructed over the trail in many places but the snow hides their exact location and we often sink into mud. Yet we are treated to such visual delights that the children are stirred to sing as they plough along. It may have been horrible yesterday but this is fun.

Few sights in nature are more beautiful than fresh snow glinting on tree and tussock at sunrise with a mountain rising in a clear sky as a backdrop. And there are few better experiences on a journey than happy companions cavorting and laughing in sheer pleasure. There are snowball fights, giggles, more snowball fights and ambushes along the trail.

The snow hangs heavy on the beech trees we pass through and a strategic tap brings it showering down on a victim. Later, as the sun does its work, revenge is sweet when the snow falls from the trees without any coaxing.

adventure log

GETTING THERE: The Round the Mountain Track can include the Northern Circuit or you can start at Waihohonu, off SH 1.

WALKING TIME: A full Round the Mountain Circuit may take anything up to a week but you can break it into comfortable journeys of around three days each – and spend several years completing the trip.

MAP: Tongariro Parkmap 273-04.

FURTHER INFORMATION: Use the DOC information brochures on the trail. Consult DOC at the Whakapapa field centre 0-7-892 3729 for track and weather conditions. VOLCANOES OF THE SOUTH WIND: A FIELD GUIDE TO THE LANDSCAPE OF TONGARIRO NATIONAL PARK by Karen Williams will help you prepare for your journey.

At times we just stop and stare, stunned by the magic, thankful to be there. You have time for that on a journey. Still, it is a relieved party that reaches the Ohakune mountain road after 4^1/$_2$ hours of walking. We are tired but happy as well – until we get home, when blisters, a bruised knee and swollen ankle are revealed to Mum, along with a graphic account of our three-day epic.

Son is delivered a hot-water bottle on demand, Daughter gets breakfast in bed – and Dad gets a flea in his ear.

up the creek

Deep in the heart of Northland's Puketi Forest, Camp Creek joins the gently flowing Waipapa River. The small creek is presumably so called because a little way above the confluence there is one of the few flat areas in the rugged forest.

There is no sign to tell a tramper negotiating the two-day Waipapa River Track that they have reached Camp Creek. But there are at least three circles of campfire stones among the widely spaced trees and here and there the carpet of native begonia looks a bit flattened. After 7 hours on a 7.3km track that guidebooks claim should take 4 to 5 hours, who cares where we are? Certainly not my tired companions, son and daughter aged eight and seven years respectively. As tramps go it is a fairly leisurely journey, an adventurous break from a glorious summer of swimming, fishing, surfing and kayaking at a nearby beach. But it is no doddle.

Puketi Forest, roughly lying between Kaeo and Mangamuka Bridge, is part of Northland Forest Park and is an integral element in proposals for a kauri national park. Its washboard topography of ridges and steep gullies draining into the lazily flowing Waipapa was logged for its kauri and rimu riches almost as soon as it was bought by the Crown from its Maori owners in 1859.

Puketi spars held the sails aloft on Her Majesty's gunships in the 19th century and kauri was still being milled at Lanes Mill in Totara North in the late 1970s to build fine racing yachts. Logs were flushed down the Waipapa into the Hokianga Harbour for more than 50 years. Gumdiggers roamed over the forest and bled living trees until 1952, when the Forest Service started logging again. Rimu was felled until 1975, by which time there was no longer enough left for a sustained cut. Kauri fell to the chainsaw for another four years. Its saviour was the discovery of a large population of the rare kokako.

Our guidebooks are Euan and Jennie Nicol's *Tramping in North Island Forest Parks* and the Automobile Association's *Guide to Tramping and Bushwalking in New Zealand*. Their information coincides. On past experience denoted tramping times err on the conservative and are well within the capabilities of carefully managed youngsters.

But the summer heat penetrates too fiercely through the thinly regenerating forest of an old logging road that heads down a ridge into a river valley. When the hour it is supposed to take to reach the Puruwharawhara Stream long since passes, we give up and stop for lunch – as it turns out, only a few minutes short of the stream.

Our first 'wire bridge crossing' (Nicols) or 'wire-rope crossing' (AA) comes as a bit of a surprise, for it consists of just two wires stretched across the divide. Still, we can easily scramble down and over the creek, as we do so for the next four such 'bridges' we come across. The next one is our first encounter with the Waipapa River. The infant river is barely more than a creek but there is a deep pool next to the crossing and the children strip for a refreshing dip and a welcome break from the trail. This quickly raises their spirits.

We cross the river twice more before leaving the damp nikau and taraire forest and the gentle contours of the valley floor to make the only real climb of the journey. Track markers are sometimes hard to find and several times we have to retrace our steps. Markers left by possum trappers add to the confusion and the track has not seen any maintenance for years. Slips and fallen trees regularly block the trail and the children have to be assisted over many. The few track signs have mostly fallen over and badly need replacing.

On the ridge that overlooks the Merumeru Falls there is evidence of another sort of destruction. In the kauri groves, huge and stately trees bear the sickening mark of gum bleeders. Licensed gum collectors worked in Puketi until 1952. So did poachers, who made deep cuts into the butts of trees for about a quarter of their circumference. Disease now infects the stems and much of the wood is rotten. One day these giants too will topple across the track.

In contrast there is no sign of human debris at Camp Creek. But one of the tidy trampers who have preceded us has left some newspaper carefully placed in a plastic bag so that it will remain dry. We wash away our sweat, change into dry clothes and have a fire going and dinner cooking in no time.

No, there are no bears, and wild pigs will not bother you either. But stupid Daddy has brought just the tent fly and it gives no protection against hordes of sparrow-sized mosquitoes. With their faces lathered in insect repellent the children sleep while Daddy spends much of the night throwing rocks and bits of wood at a procession of possums that clatter through the pots and plates. One of the stupidly destructive creatures races off through the dying fire. Serves him right too.

adventure log

GETTING THERE: The Waipapa River Track starts at the Puketi Forest recreation area on Waiare Road, between SH 10 and SH 1. It exits at the Forest Pools picnic area just off SH 1.

WALKING TIME: Two days should get you from start to finish of this 20km tramp.

MAP: LINZ P05.

FURTHER INFORMATION: DOC has an information brochure on Puketi Forest. Also see TRAMPING IN NORTH ISLAND FOREST PARKS by Euan and Jennie Nicol and AA GUIDE TO TRAMPING AND BUSHWALKING IN NEW ZEALAND. DOC Kerikeri field centre 0-9-407 8474.

In the morning the children filter fresh water while I break camp. It is difficult to believe that these crystal-clear streams are any less wonderful to drink than they were in my youth but there are giardia warning signs at park headquarters so why risk it?

With some protestations my companions change into their damp clothing from the previous day. But soon we have again reached the Waipapa River. There is not a sign in sight as the track descends to the river. It would be a miracle if a party making the journey the other way spotted two tiny tree blazes about 2m apart and partly obscured by foliage.

From here the route is billed as 5km in the bed of the river, which should take about 2^1/$_2$ hours. The bush-clad hills rise steeply from the river yet the Waipapa has a gentle fall and has long provided human access into the depths of the forest. The walk is not recommended in rain but there is no warning that even in good times the bed of the river sometimes gets a good deal lower than the level of the water. The children think their first swim with their rucksacks across a deep pool is 'awesome'.

The scenery certainly is. In low flow the Waipapa barely moves. The deep pools are a rich, alluring contrast with the clean gravel beds. Thick bush fringes the river banks and bright red dragonflies dart across the water. Bullies and koura are easily spotted in the shallows; bird song is a constant companion.

After a couple of hours the novelty begins to wear off. Wading and swimming is tiring and the river twists and turns so much that the children are convinced that we are going around in circles. They also begin to feel cold so, stripped of their wet shirts, they lie in the sun on hot rocks beside the river until they warm again.

We spend 5 hours negotiating the river 'bed'. Lunch is sodden. So are the kids' sleeping bags because Daddy has a plastic liner for his own pack but not the children's rucksacks. The penalty for this is to carry their gear, and seemingly half the Waipapa River too.

The route leaves the Waipapa at its junction with the Mangapa River and follows what was once an old logging road out of the forest. It is flat but overgrown and the way is often blocked by fallen trees and slips. The Waipapa is a constant companion and through the trees I spy long, deep pools that I promise one day I will return to with a trout rod.

But for the moment I am too busy cajoling and encouraging two of the most tired and gutsy kids you will find. Bare feet on a moss-covered road at least gives relief from blisters. When finally we hear voices of people swimming at the Forest Pools picnic area my daughter demands to re-shoulder her pack. She intends to finish the adventure as she began it, as a tramper. It is 8 hours and 15km since we left Camp Creek; we are $3^1/2$ hours late for our rendezvous with an anxious but relieved mother.

Next day the children swim, surf and play on the beach with their usual relaxed abandon. Daddy hobbles around the campsite on legs feeling a few twinges from 5 hours of river wading. Serves him right too.

Note: Since our journey, the wire rope crossings have been removed in line with DOC policy on safety, and work has begun on upgrading the track and improving the trail marking.

eight kilometres as the kereru flies

Explorers usually have good reason for the lyrical names they impose on the landscape. They don't call places Roaring Lion River, Beehive Island, Jagged Peak or Guano Island for nothing. So a modern adventurer following in their footsteps should be a little curious about a river the Maori named Hoteo.

The river rises in the Wayby valley, east of Wellsford, and the tentacles of various streams that feed it reach almost to the coast near Te Arai Point. But the Hoteo owes its name to the way it carves west to the Kaipara Harbour. Somewhere around the heights of Dills Road a long-ago explorer with an eye for form saw the shape of a large calabash or gourd etched into the bush. A map shows the accuracy of the description and indicates why we plan to take a leisurely two days on a journey that is just 8km in a straight line.

The Hoteo barely rates a mention in river-running guidebooks but others have long valued it. There are several pa sites along its flanks and European colonists used it as the main line of communication in the settlement of the Kaipara hills and flats. Those who farm the land cleared from the bush know that the calabash is often filled with mullet, whitebait and wild fowl.

A friend raised in these hills, just an hour from Auckland, suggested a paddle around the calabash. Canoe clubs sometimes make a long single day of a trip down the Hoteo but we plan a casual family adventure in Canadian canoes with an overnight stop at a riverside bach. Using Canadians for the first time adds an extra element of adventure. This may not be the mighty Hudson or the Yukon but there is an unmistakable flavour of wilderness as we pack our provisions in dry bags and barrels and stow them in the canoes.

We begin at the old settlement of Hoteo. I have been warned that keeping a Canadian on the straight and narrow can test happy relationships but the sleek machine I have borrowed causes no problems. It has a pronounced Indian-style bow and stern and I keep thinking that I should be in buckskins and a Davy Crockett hat with a load of furs on board.

We keep a sharp watch out for danger lurking behind the trees and in the undergrowth. The cows just give a curious stare and the attack when it comes is from our companions. Who can resist a golf swing that sends a divot of water at the crew of a passing canoe? One thing leads to another, of course. At close quarters, with no holds barred, a large plastic bailer is a more suitable weapon, capable of sending litres of water over the enemy. A large, bicycle pump-like bailer – and I have one – has even better fire-power and cannons out such a stream of water that the attacking savages have to stop and empty out their canoe. Dry bags and barrels have their uses on even the gentlest of rivers.

adventure log

GETTING THERE: Start at Hoteo River bridge on SH1 between Warkworth and Wellsford – or even further upstream at the Wayby Valley – or downstream at Hoteo on the Warkworth–Tauhoa Road. Exit at SH 16.

PADDLING TIME: A long, long day or a comfortable two-day journey – with landowner permission to camp.

MAP: LINZ Q09.

FURTHER INFORMATION: This is a forgotten river so paddling it is a journey of exploration.

The outline of a calabash – the river actually carves at least three calabash shapes – is through farmland but there are frequent patches of bush on the banks, predominantly of manuka and totara. At several places where the river widens into pools there are duck shooters' maimais hidden in the foliage.

No one could suggest the Hoteo is a sparkling mountain stream; its water is more like tea than gin. But it compensates for that by delivering a tranquillity as good as any in the wilderness. Two rapids, Paraua and Tarakihi, are big enough to bear the name but at the water flow we encounter they are less troublesome than a bailer of water wielded at close quarters. Perhaps we should count ourselves lucky. There is debris lodged in tree branches 6m to 7m higher than the water level. When in flood the Hoteo must flow furiously.

Parana is a shelf of rock stretching across the river. It stops the sea water from the Kaipara Harbour from going much further upstream. We are fortunate to have the use of a bach here. It sits in one of the calabashes, on an enviable peninsula of land bounded by the Hoteo. Across the river there is thick native bush. Downstream, and easily reached by runabout at high tide, are the fishing grounds of the Kaipara Harbour. Old pear trees around the bach are doubtless the legacy of a settler who travelled upstream as far as the tide goes.

We wake to a chorus of magpies and tui and wait for the tide to turn before paddling on. Soon the river widens, mangroves line its banks – and a jetskier roars around a bend to break our tranquillity and bring us back to reality.

a raftful of fun

A helicopter follows the sliver of the upper Mohaka River as it slices erratically through the dappled beech forest of the Kaweka Forest Park, south-east of Lake Taupo. It clatters down to a small shingle island just big enough to inflate a couple of rubber rafts and hold assorted camping gear and a knot of slightly stunned people who have been brought in on earlier loads.

Then it is gone, back to its base near Poronui Station on the edge of the rugged Kaimanawa Forest Park, where the Mohaka began its journey and to where the chopper usually ferries trophy trout fishermen and hunters after the area's famed sika deer.

On the shingle island there is nervous silence. This is a family outdoor adventure, with ages ranging from eight to 49, but the excitement has begun with a breathless suddenness, as if plunging into a freezing pool. Faces are set in a grin from the helicopter ride. Just over an hour ago we were in the civilisation of Taupo. Now we are in the middle of an isolated river in a subalpine beech forest. The only other signs of life are insects hovering over the fast-flowing water, and some that take an occasional nip out of an exposed ankle.

All is anticipation; the future is unknown even if golden beech leaves floating on the river surface show in which direction it lies. But first there are some more immediate things to do. Rafting guides Simon Dixon and Noel Rusden get us organised inflating rafts, repacking watertight barrels and stowing our gear on board.

Dixon runs a company that takes people, often family groups, on canoe safaris down the Whanganui River. It is mainly a leisurely, relaxing river cruise using Canadian canoes. Rusden, one of the country's most experienced rafting guides, takes rafting safaris down the wet, and sometimes wild, but always scenically spectacular Motu River. Neither man has children – which may be why they have put their heads together to come up with an exciting wilderness tour for Mum, Dad and the kids.

Dixon dreamt up an intermediate river trip, a step up from the Whanganui, that would introduce people to whitewater, be suitable for families with young children but still be exciting. Young children are usually excluded from commercial whitewater rafting, but they are welcome on the mainly grade-two rapids of the upper Mohaka.

The Mohaka begins in the Kaimanawa Forest Park at the junction of the Oamaru and Kaipo Rivers, about 3 hours of rafting further upstream from where we have landed. But the river in this section can be shallow in low flows. There are also access difficulties further upstream because of land ownership. Hence the helicopter and the dramatic plunge into adventure.

The rafts, which are to be our caravans for three days, are carefully packed. One carries two large barrels beneath which a net holds fruit, vegetables and liquid refreshments kept chilled by the water rushing underneath the raft. The children find the barrels perfect for straddling in ride 'em cowboy mode as we lurch down the rapids. The other raft is loaded high with camping equipment and waterproof barrels of personal gear. There is a third inflatable that is an inspired bit of thinking on Dixon's part. It is a two-person inflatable kayak that tags along as a speedy outrider to the rafts carrying our gear.

We don our helmets and life-jackets, slide the rafts into the water and paddle off. On the upper Mohaka the rafting instructions are simple: forward paddle, back paddle, and rest. The grins are still fixed but the stunned silence is fading. A few paddling mix-ups, a splash or two with the paddle blade, and we very quickly become one big happy family.

Apart from their size, there is soon not a lot to distinguish the kids from the grown-ups. When we stop for a drinks break beside a large rock and a deep pool, the adults climb the rock to 'bomb' the small kayak.

We lunch in the sun on a shingle beach, a spread laid out before us on a fold-up table. There are deer prints in the sand. The children watch tiny fish in the shallows, and try their hand at paddling the inflatable kayak. In the afternoon I take my children in the kayak. It is reassuringly stable through the rapids yet exciting – and often wet, too. Older children could handle the kayak on their own – so long as they could persuade their parents to get out of it. I have never paddled whitewater before but soon find that on this grade of rapid – and with the benefit of following an experienced raft guide – that the technique comes quite easily.

We reach the Mangatainoka hot springs campsite in late afternoon. It is a large, well-used camping area. The metal luggage frame inside one raft con-verts to a table for cooking and preparing food. A large tent fly is rigged over the dining area. The children choose a spot to pitch a tent, lay out the sleeping bags, then go exploring – while their parents enjoy a blissful nap.

The more energetic in the party are out in the inflatable kayak, repeatedly running the rapid just below the campsite. They don't mind if they get wet because what makes this camp particularly special is the drain-sized stream that spews hot water out of the hill behind. A nifty downpipe system catches the water and fills two spa-sized baths that are surrounded by wooden decking and seats. The baths – emptied when you leave – are rigged to begin filling when you first arrive so that they are ready for an evening spa.

There are stars overhead and glow-worms in the bank behind the baths. The Mohaka tumbles on noisily in the background as you sit up to your neck in natural hot water. It is excessively indulgent but we are getting used to being pampered. Our dessert that night is ice cream and fruit salad – and you can be sure that no one walking to this remote spot eats like that.

Next morning we are still loading the rafts when two walkers arrive from a couple of hours downstream. They are young Project Green workers who are on track maintenance and working as hut wardens at Te Puia Lodge. We stop at the riverside lodge for morning tea. A Napier father and his two young boys are passing on their way up to the hot springs for the night. They shoulder heavy packs with a smile as Dad leads them out.

A track runs alongside the river but rafters have the advantage of access to both sides. We stop for lunch at a rafters' camp that, apart from being wonderfully remote, is alongside an ideal rapid for the children to back-float on using their life-jackets for buoyancy. Further downstream is Mangatutu hot springs, set in the cliff face above the river. This one is accessible by four-wheel-drive vehicle and it tends to show in the debris left around and in the picnic area fencing that has been used for a bonfire.

We camp that night on the remote side of the river and dine on steak grilled over an open fire. We play cards and roast marshmallows, sip wine, enjoy new friendships and think how lucky we are.

Trout disdain the lures we throw at them but we do have pancakes for breakfast. We have dropped a lot in altitude and it is warmer now. The forest changes and kowhai line the river bank. Yesterday we saw a blue duck; today we see parries. The river is joined by the Ripia River and we run a couple of larger rapids. We stop for lunch by the best of them so the big kids can run it several times in the inflatable kayak.

By mid-afternoon we are at the take-out point near the Napier–Taupo Road. It is the end of a very special three-day family adventure but it is also just the beginning. Wife and children insist there must be others to follow. Simon Dixon's introduction to wilderness rafting has given the family a taste for it.

a swell time?

Back in the 4th century BC Aristotle suggested that means are more important than ends. Other philosophers just as readily proclaim that it is the destination that counts, not the journey. Sea kayakers fall into both philosophical camps. So when I am asked what I enjoy best about paddling my canoe – or wearing out tramping-boot leather – I have no hesitation in disagreeing with that ancient Greek. Often the best part of the day is sitting around an evening campsite, no matter how you get there.

The cause of this ethical discourse on outdoor pursuits is the Oceans Sea-Kayak Classic at Matauri Bay and a wind-down paddle up the coast. The Matauri Classic is one of those wonderful events that transcends do-or-die competitive racing. You can be sure that most of the mixed bag of entrants who paddle sea kayaks for 34km or so round the Cavalli Islands would wholeheartedly endorse Aristotle's sentiments.

These islands, with their mix of open water, sheltered passages, quiet bays and craggy reefs, were created for kayak cruising. And there can be no better way to gain cruising confidence under all conditions than to compete in an event like the Classic.

Outside Motutapere Island conflicting swells create small waterspouts and it seems the only thing to stop a capsize is to keep paddling. The experience will prove beneficial. Four hours and a bit later – well after the young-gun racers – we slide onto the beach at Putataua Bay and the welcome hospitality of Dover and Jackie Samuels. At the prize-giving I win a spot prize of a hammock, which seems philosophically appropriate.

But having proved that body and kayak can handle these seas, it is time to go cruising. Three Cavalli-hardened singles and a double manned by two youths paddle north in spring sunshine. The breeze is across our bows at about north-west, instead of the forecast north-easterlies that would have nicely pushed us along from behind. Still, a laden kayak is a stable joy compared with the cork that we raced around the Cavallis the day before.

The main problem is that the double has more windage and, with a stiffening breeze coming across their forward quarter and seas becoming more lumpy and disturbed, the boys are having difficulty keeping on track. As we head around the first major headland, Opounui Point, the wind whips into our faces in gusts that the boys, who have been paddling the kayak for less than an hour, neither enjoy nor cope with well. When my son tells me he is more unhappy than he has ever been on a frightening clifftop, I call a general retreat and we duck back to the shelter of a small bay just inside the point. It is time for a snack and a chance for the boys to regain their composure.

When we paddle on again I secure a tow rope to the bow of the double. It helps keep the bow into the wind and gives the young paddlers the confidence to tackle seas around the point that if anything have got worse. In these conditions there is nothing to do but keep paddling because even with the smallest break the wind will have us scooting back and waste gruelling metres that we have clawed out against it.

Far in the distance is a green roof on the foreshore and that is where we head. We are almost on the shore of the most delightful beach imaginable before we finally get some shelter from the furious gusts and the aquamarine water stills and clears. The roof belongs to the only home on this orange-sand cove just north of Wainui Bay. On this day they have to share their paradise with a group that has worked hard to get there and deserves to laze in such a beautiful, sunny lunch spot.

Mahinepua Bay is rated as one of the finest anchorages in Northland but it is covered by a nasty chop as we cross to the peninsula and run along the shore towards Motuekaiti and Flat Islands. We know it is going to be tough when we get around the point but decide to see for ourselves. We sneak through convenient gaps in the reef before hitting the full force of the wind, now gusting about 25 knots and picking up spume and throwing it straight in our faces.

It is far from pleasant. We are on a lee shore that is a mass of vicious rocks and white foam, and at our rate of progress it is going to take a couple of hours to reach our planned camping spot. Peter Sommerhalder draws on his considerable experience and turns us around. The experts might call this risk management, but common sense will do. If the boys had capsized – a distinct possibility in these frighteningly confused seas – we would have faced a particularly difficult rescue.

We retreat to a sheltered beach in Mahinepua Bay and pitch our tents just above high-water mark. This whole region is peppered with pa sites and there are six just on this tiny peninsula, which is a reserve within the Bay of Islands

Maritime Park. A well-marked track that runs along the spine of the peninsula yields panoramic views. To the west is the huge Whangaroa Bay and to the east the Cavalli group. As if on cue, a square-rigger, perhaps the R. Tucker Thompson, glides in to anchor in Mahinepua Bay.

We are treated next morning to dazzling sunrise over the bay. A pod of dolphins wishes us good fortune as we paddle off early to beat the usual mid-morning sea breeze. Our tumult of the day before is now a near-glassy swell and we glide through the gaps in the reef with huge smiles instead of grimaces.

In less than half an hour we are at our turnaround point and heading for a cluster of rocks marked by the distinctive Frenchman Rock. In the comfort of these conditions we take full advantage of our narrow craft and pass through short-cuts that are barred to most other vessels.

Just ahead is Oruatemanu Island and Arrow Rocks, and nowhere is the delight of sea kayaking more evident than when we bear slightly to starboard to make landfall. Boating guides to the region use words like 'ugly', 'hazard' and 'foul ground', advising craft to keep well clear. Instead we safely negotiate the reefs that rise from nowhere, and glide into a small beach.

We have a particular reason for landing because on this tiny island is the most spectacular example of primeval sedimentary layering that you can ever hope to see. Each layer is only a few centimetres thick and almost all are a different colour. As well, the layers have been folded and twisted by vast geological forces. Nature's canvas on this small island surpasses anything the imagination of a human artist can achieve.

That, however, is not the finale to our small cruise. Past Tauranga Bay lies the narrow entrance to Whangaroa Harbour and a clutch of caves treasured by Maori imagination and kayak adventurers. On the south head is Popoko-Maui, an elaborate cave that is like the entrance to the human gullet, with tonsillar folds and a uvula. It is the throat of Maui, and here is imprisoned the fierce and unpredictable east wind that may blow rarely but does with fury.

Today it is well and truly trapped and we can paddle right into Maui's stomach, where the slight swell sends out a resonant echo as it washes against the rear of the cave. A little further on is a narrower cave whose entrance is guarded by the hanging root of a pohutukawa, perhaps 30m long, and down which runs a small waterfall. It is a chance for the cousins in the double to indulge in youthful games and ensure each takes a shower on the way in and out of the cave.

On the north head is the large cave of Ure-Maui, in which Whangaroa imprisons the relatively docile west wind. Long ago the roof of the cave fell so the westerly can escape to become the prevailing wind. The open roof is like a huge clear dome, framed by trees, that draws gasps of 'awesome' from our paddlers.

Further north is Jellicoe Cave, a route so narrow that paddle blades scrape against its sides. It is a double-ended cave that cuts a passage through a considerable chunk of rocky coastline. The Hole-in-the-Wall does much the same but it is wider, shorter and higher so that on a good day runabouts will bravely charge through too.

Taupo Bay, our destination, is just around the corner. By now our epic of the day before is a distant memory. Young nephew walks ashore and greets his aunt with the words, 'Aunty Fran, they tried to kill us yesterday.'

Aristotle would be pleased.

adventure log

GETTING THERE: The kayaking paradise of the Cavalli Islands is reached from the Matauri Bay Road off SH 10.

PADDLING TIME: Anything from 1 day to 5.

MARINE CHART: 5121.

FURTHER INFORMATION: See SEA KAYAKER'S GUIDE TO NEW ZEALAND'S UPPER NORTH ISLAND by Vincent Maire, Royal Akarana Yacht Club Coastal Cruising Handbook and THE NORTHLAND COAST: A BOATMAN'S GUIDE by William Owen. Guided tours with New Zealand Sea Kayak Adventures 0-9-402 8596.

WHANGAREI

Waipu Caves   Great Barrier
                Island
Kaipara
Harbour   Mahurangi Harbour

              AUCKLAND
                THAMES

                    TAURANGA

              HAMILTON
                    ROTORUA

                    TAUPO
NEW PLYMOUTH   TURANGI   GISBORNE
                Tongariro   Tongariro
                National   River   Mahia
                Park   Peninsula
                                NAPIER/
                                HASTINGS
                    WANGANUI

                PALMERSTON
                NORTH

WELLINGTON

any means to an end

There are so many different ways to get into the outdoors. You don't have to tramp with a heavy pack through impenetrable bush or paddle against the tide. You can enjoy it sitting on your backside on a bike or in a dinghy, sliding on a pair of skis or holding a fishing rod. You don't even have to leave the city – there are plenty of adventures to be had in leafy suburbia.

walking in a winter wonderland

According to the small thermometer on my jacket it is −10°C – but nature refuses to take that into account. There are three of us, snug in a tent that is generously classified as two-to-three persons but whose makers neglected to suggest that it helps to be skinny. Chris and Martin are skinny. Chris has his sleeping bag hood drawn tight so that only his nose and eyes are visible. Ice has formed on the roof of the inner tent from the condensation of our breath.

I can ignore the call of nature no longer and struggle out of my cosy pit, trying not to kneel on Martin as I unzip the tent door. The huge expanse of South Crater, which separates Mt Ngauruhoe from Mt Tongariro, is bathed in a pale blue light. A torch is superfluous under a near-full moon, as white as the mantle on a Tilley lamp. Ice crystals around our tent mimic the twinkling stars above.

To the south the bulk of Ngauruhoe is cleanly etched on the skyline; to the north is the summit of Mt Tongariro. I have seen something like this before, in the ghostly light of polar documentaries. The clarity is as sharp as the chill that is just starting to seep into my sleepy consciousness.

'You guys have just got to look at this,' I urge, knowing that I must have woken them getting out of my sack. 'It's like being in the Antarctic. A mumbled response suggests they will take my word for it. Still, I am glad nature called, albeit frostily, and even gladder to be here.

Tongariro National Park can be sublime ski-touring country, with a distinctive character and surprising variety. On the Ruapehu massif there are glacial slopes that reward energetic tourists with descents on broad ski-highways. And between the peaks of Ruapehu, Tongariro and Ngauruhoe is a jumbled topography of craters, valleys and hillocks that in midwinter snow makes an ideal playground for those who want to ski the back country.

There is one problem; the weather can be diabolical, which means the snow conditions can be too. So when the forecast is reasonable you go for it. We head into the Mangatepopo valley, an old glacial valley and the route for the Tongariro Crossing. I have walked it in both summer and winter – and I still prefer it under a soothing white mantle.

Low cloud obscures Ngauruhoe and there is a chill breeze but the snow, which we soon reach, offers firm and easy walking. The headwall of the valley is a severely steep way to start a weekend in the hills. On my first visit here a companion called the section the 'gutbuster' and, as clichéd as the description might be, it is nonetheless appropriate.

By the time I pant my way onto South Crater and join the others, the weather has cleared. The expanse is not a crater at all but, enclosed on three sides, it gives the impression of being one. The fourth side is the valley we have just walked up and in clear weather it gives a viewing corridor all the way to Mt Taranaki. At present it is a wind funnel so we walk on and find some shelter under a low bank before pitching our tent.

To tent or not to tent tends to be a ski tourist's dilemma. Tents mean weight to carry whereas a snow cave can be built on the spot. The trouble is that it takes about 2 hours to build an adequate snow shelter and in this region there is always a worry as to whether the snow will be deep enough.

The first winter I ski toured here I sheltered from a storm in a snug snow cave. Inside, the wind was barely audible and sleep came easily. Too easily, perhaps. The sun was well up when it shone through our ventilation hole like a torch beam. By the time we broke out of our warm refuge a group of skiers had made it up the gutbuster and halfway up Ngauruhoe, their 'yahoos' in ecstasy at a gloriously clear and sunny morning floating reproachfully across South Crater. As it turns out the bank behind which we shelter on this trip would have been perfect for a cave too – but with a tent up, we have other things to do.

No one can drive past Mt Ngauruhoe without being enticed by its perfect andesite cone form. Its slopes demand to be skied. So with climbing skins attached to our skis we begin a slow trudge to the summit. Wind and rain have turned the snow into marbled ice that the skins have difficulty gripping. When the ice lumps reach tennis-ball size we don crampons and shoulder our skis.

The climb to the 2287m summit tends to be a plod, perhaps because there is little terrain variation that would encourage attention to wander and time to pass. But the view expands in direct proportion to the height. Above 1900m we can look across the Red Crater saddle to Lake Taupo. To the east lies the Desert Road and the snow-capped Kaimanawa Range. Far below is the speck of our tent.

On the summit a few trampers enjoy what is left of the afternoon sun but it is late and even softer snow patches have already frozen hard. If this was packed powder the skiing would be superb. Instead it is ice that threatens to dislodge teeth as you chatter down it. A slope that took nearly 3 hours to get up is skied down in less than 15 minutes, stops included. The next day a tramper we meet tells me that we had made an impressive fist of skiing down. 'Could you see us?' I ask. 'Actually, we could hear you,' he replies.

In the morning Chris declares that he will get up when the sun hits our tent, so Martin unzips the flap and the sun shines straight into Chris's face. The ridge up to Red Crater, however, is in shadow and likely to be that way for a few hours. I theorise that it will be too icy to skin up on our skis and follow a skiing Martin in my crampons. He soon pulls ahead and seems to have no trouble so I switch to skis – just as he switches to crampons.

Halfway up the slope I lose all traction and slide to the bottom, narrowly missing a couple of large rocks on the way. I lose a bit of skin but the bigger wound is to my pride; the slide is in full view of a tramping club group equipped with climbing helmets and ice axes.

This has now become a challenge. With the help of crampon-like devices attached to my skis I breast the ridge – and switch to walking crampons. At 1am the view had been ethereal. Now it is pure magic. Ngauruhoe dominates a richly blue sky. The cone of Mt Taranaki appears on the far skyline like an iceberg. To the north lies the flat pan of Central Crater and Lake Taupo. To the east is the Oturere valley, which looks great for ski touring too, and the Kaimanawa and Ruahine Ranges. Two days is just not long enough here; there are hectares of snow to be skinned up and skied down – next time.

I let out a 'yahoo' on the ski descent into the crater just to show off to the trampers and get up enough speed to get two-thirds of the way across the crater before slowly sliding to a halt. When I look back the trampers are specks on the skyline.

We ski all the way to Ketetahi Hut before softening snow runs out and I am stopped dead by a tussock clump that deals yet more damage to ageing knees. Far below is Lake Rotoaira and in the distance, across the thickly forested Pihanga, is Lake Taupo.

It is still a good 2 hours to the car park off the Rangipo Road, down past the Ketetahi hot springs and through the tussock shrubland to the lush podocarp-hardwood forest that sits like an apron on the north of Tongariro. In two days we have traversed from alpine scrub and old lava flows to thermal springs and a rain forest; across long-dead volcanic craters and past a still active one. When you can do that mostly on skis and on perfect snow, it must be the best two-day ski tour in the country.

horsing around in east coast style

'Don't laugh,' says Ray Thompson as he rather sheepishly carries his hunting clothes into his bedroom to get changed.

The raw-boned farmer from Tunanui Station, near Wairoa, who rides a horse for work and pleasure is no John Peel, the legendary Cumberland huntsman of last century with his 'coat so gay'. Thompson's coat is the green with yellow collar of the Mahia Hunt and he is a tad self-conscious about his tight white riding breeches, white shirt and long silk scarf, which his daughter Amy helps him to tie.

But Peel, who ran a pack of hounds for 40 years, would surely enjoy a day with this hunt and hounds, one of the oldest packs in the country (it started in 1885) even if there are no foxes to send running from their lairs. The Mahia Hunt, like others in New Zealand, chases hares, or at least that is the excuse. It soon becomes obvious when I accept an invitation to join the annual hunt on the Maori-owned Onenui Station on the end of the Mahia Peninsula that hares have little to do with the activity. It's all about horses with the hounds – never call them dogs – rating a distant second and the hares rarely mentioned at all.

The pre-hunt conversation is about the quality of the jumps at the hunt's last outing and how many were taken, how a certain horse performed in comparison with another, and how well various members of the hunt may have ridden – the thrill of the chase and that sort of stuff. Frankly, I find all this horse-jumping talk more frightening than the thought of a hare being ripped to shreds. I am assured that using gates is perfectly acceptable, but does my horse know that?

As a child I used to visit an uncle's farm near the Waipoua kauri forest and head off for the day on Red, all the time pretending I was a cowboy. At a canter Red gave unnerving little jumps that my uncle called 'pig jumps'. The Thompson horses are better schooled than that. I'm on Mustang Sally, a grey pony that belongs to Amy, who shares her father's passion for horses.

Onenui Station, at the end of the flat-topped Mahia Peninsula, is noted for its horses. It is also made for them with long, rolling paddocks on the high land and views of the Pacific Ocean from almost any vantage point. Onenui and its station manager, Brian 'Bruno' Lloyd, have been preparing for the annual hunt, lowering fences and making space in the shearers' quarters for some members of the hunt to stay the night and for the hunt 'breakfast'.

It is one of the peculiarities of hunting that the breakfast is not a breakfast at all. It's more like a late lunch that you have when the hunt is over. What we have now is some fruit cake and port to fortify our spirits. It is a tradition at Mahia, which draws its riders from far afield.

The scene around the yards looks much like the collection of vehicles, floats, trucks and horses at a Pony Club meet. The difference is that the riders come in every shape, size, age, gender and occupation – until transformed by their hunting coats into a hunt to make John Peel proud. There are farmers, school teachers and lawyers. The one thing they have in common is a passion for riding horses.

The Master of the Hunt, Dave Withers, has the face of a friendly grandfather and the physique and hands of a man who has worked hard all his life and had a few scrapes along the way. He farms near Lake Waikaremoana and is a fearless and consummate horseman, riding in the show-jumping ring, the hunt, at polo and around his farm. Decades of doing that on all sorts of horses can take its toll and Withers has had his share of broken bones.

That, however, does not stop him from using Shanks's pony, with a pack on his back, to every nook and cranny of the Urewera. He knows the park tracks so well that he is the first call for search-and-rescue operations and comes to the hunt fresh from yet another call-out to find a lost tramper.

Morning tea over, Withers calls his 'field' together and gives the day's riding instructions, outlining where fences have been lowered and pitfalls he has found on a preliminary ride around the area.

Thompson explains the game plan to me. I don't understand much of the detail but the basic idea is that the huntsman, who is paid by the hunt to look after its hounds, the master and his two assistants (whips) let the hounds try to find the scent of a hare. If they do, the chase is on to follow them. It is not totally harum scarum. The hunt master is responsible for the safety of the hunt and must lead it on a route that it is reasonable for others to follow.

His whips help the huntsman to control the hounds, keeping them to their task – they may be hounds but they can act like mischievous dogs – and ensuring they do not venture into out-of-bounds areas that the landowner

adventure log

GETTING THERE: The Mahia Peninsula is off SH 2 between Wairoa and Gisborne.

BE INSPIRED: Horse-riding is not everyone's bag but there are good opportunities in the region for a wide range of outdoor pursuits, particularly surfing and fishing. You can also go horse trekking at Wainui, north of Gisborne.

FURTHER INFORMATION: First Light Tourism in Gisborne has one of the most comprehensive information centres you can find. For more information go to 0-6-868 6139, www.eastlandtourism.co.nz and 0-6-867 2000, www.gisborne.govt.nz. Also DOC Gisborne 0-6-868 6139.

may have requested the hunt to keep clear of. At the same time there is huge scope for the daring to tackle the higher road and the scared witless like me to find a gate that will open.

Two or three others are following my course but Mustang Sally is none too happy about such a boring route while the other horses are having so much fun. She's prancing and flinging her head around at the tight rein I am putting on. Eventually she protests with a couple of bucks and I decide to keep my dignity intact. Thompson's wife, Leslie, and Amy have been following the hunt in a four-wheel-drive vehicle. Amy needs little persuasion to quickly don her hunting jacket, swap seats and set her horse free to jump with the others. I'm happy with another port.

Eventually Withers calls it a day. There have been no hares but the field is more than happy with the ride and the quality of the jumps. Back at the shearers' quarters they tuck into good East Coast food while the huntsman feeds his happy hounds.

just in time for breakfast

At 6.30am it is barely light on the Tongariro River. Turangi still seems to be asleep but there is already an angler in a choice spot in the Boulder Pool, so fishing guide Tim McCarthy takes me to the Breakfast Pool. It is in the centre of town and one of the most accessible fishing pools on this famed trout river but we have it all to ourselves. The pool was given its name because anglers from the houses behind it could fish for an hour and catch a trout before breakfast.

McCarthy knows it better as a lunch pool because as a schoolboy he used to rush there as soon as the school lunch bell rang. If the fishing was halfway decent he would stay there for the afternoon. Sometimes a teacher would even give him permission – so long as McCarthy dropped a trout off that evening. McCarthy learned his lessons and now makes a living showing other people where to catch trout.

Years ago I took my first river trout from here, wet fly fishing at dusk, although I would hesitate to show anyone a photograph of it. In my ignorance I kept a silver, eel-like hen, totally spent from having fought her way up the Tongariro to spawn. When she lunged at my feathered imitation of a dark cockabully she was on her way back to Lake Taupo to rest and recuperate.

If a guide such as McCarthy had been with me the spent hen probably would have got there. Some years later we arranged for him to guide a friend's teenage son on his first trip to the Tongariro. They fished the Whitikau Pool and, guided to where the fish were lying, the boy soon hooked into his first river trout. As he brought it into the shallows his excitement vanished as McCarthy reached down and released the trout. It was a 'slab' or spent fish.

I am desperately in need of a different sort of lesson. I agree there is more to the calm recreation of angling than simply catching fish but it does help to maintain an interest if you succeed sometimes. And in the last couple of years I have had no success on the Tongariro.

The problem is that I have been playing at this outdoor pursuit, that some

adventure log

GETTING THERE: Turangi is at the southern end of Lake Taupo on SH 1.

FISHING SEASON: Trout start running up the Tongariro River to spawn with the onset of winter rains in May.

FURTHER INFORMATION: The staff at Sporting Life in the Turangi mall will happily advise you where and when and recommend a guide: 0-7-386 8996, www.sportinglife-turangi.co.nz. A special Taupo licence is required for the region. DOC Turangi 0-7-386 8607. See also www.ruapehunz.com.

insist is an art, flicking a line into the river at brief interludes between skiing or tramping. Fishing knowledge takes time and keen observation to acquire – or the help of a fishing guide like McCarthy. It can be frowned on in some fishing circles, but as the president of the New Zealand Professional Fishing Guides Association, Frank Murphy, explains, people think nothing of hiring a golf professional.

I know the Breakfast Pool is fishing well because the week before a colleague who is a good fisherman took home his Taupo three-fish bag limit as well as catching and releasing four other fine fish. I step into the tail of the pool. Below me is the famous Major Jones pool.

It is a test of rusty skill here because there is no room for a backcast and the line has to be sidecast. The pool is deep and shelves relatively quickly. The nymph imitation has to tumble along the bottom of the pool just where the fish are lying waiting for the current to bring them breakfast.

Every now and again I get it right. To fool a waiting trout the artificial is food, it has to tumble at the same speed as the current like any other piece of debris. If it goes slower or faster, trout will know it is false so it is important that the floating flyline does not drag or push the nymph at a different speed.

'Mend your line downstream,' McCarthy tells me, which stops my line in slower water from holding back the nymph that is tumbling along in faster water.

'Hit it, hit it!' shouts my guide, and I have a fish on the line. 'Just play it by hand, he'll probably take out the loose line, but don't let it down into the rapid or you'll lose it.'

I follow instructions and have the fish under control as McCarthy retreats up the bank to collect his landing net. Suddenly the line goes free; the hook has pulled out.

We move up the pool about 10m and I cast again. This time I see the indicator disappear and am striking at the same moment as my guide shouts 'Hit it!'

There is always a tenuous hold on any fish but nothing more so than with a soft-mouthed trout and a hook no bigger than a drawing pin. The trout runs and shakes its head angrily before it is landed. It is a hen weighing 2.75kg.

Another 10m up the pool towards the swing bridge that gives access to the particularly enjoyable Tongariro River Walk the line indicator dips again. This time the fish weighs in at 2.25kg. Further upstream and I have room to backcast. I land a third fish, a little smaller than the other two but in good condition. It puts up no fight at all and McCarthy suggests it must be near spawning.

'If you kill it that will be the end of your fishing for the day. Let it go,' he says. So I do, with no regrets. It was Turangi guides like McCarthy who pushed to have the Taupo bag limit reduced from eight fish to three. Even two is more than enough.

the unique charm of dinghy cruising

Lounging comfortably in the cockpit of a 1938 Z-class dinghy as it zips under jib towards the South Head of the Kaipara Harbour provides plenty of time for reflection. Thoughts like, Who needs an expensive Hauraki Gulf cruiser and Westhaven mooring? spring to mind. The sturdy, solid kauri *Tawaki*, a champion racing boat in her day cost $300, near-new road trailer included. And despite the several empty boat trailers at Shelly Beach this morning, the Kaipara, unlike its cousin only a few miles away, appears deserted.

Already two of the features of dinghy cruising have emerged: it is inexpensive and the most suitable waters are often those other yachtsmen ignore. In Great Britain and on the west coast of North America they have known that for a long time. There, many dinghy-cruising adherents have maintained the tradition of extended voyaging on rivers, estuaries and along the coastline in small boats powered by sail, oar or paddle. Such basic voyaging has had little following in New Zealand, yet with keel boats now beyond many people's reach and the once cheaper option of trailer-sailers having escalated in price and size, dinghy cruising offers a viable alternative to those who still dream of going down to the sea or river.

Dinghy cruising combines a wide range of outdoor skills, from seamanship to camping, natural history and a keen appreciation of the vagaries of tide and weather. Perhaps most enticing of all, it revives the child in us. Each journey is a voyage of exploration to waters often teeming with both history and wildlife where fancy cruisers would never dare to venture. Few cruising grounds are beyond the reach of the small-boat voyager – and New Zealand contains many ideal waters, from the sounds of Marlborough to the many small harbours and estuaries of Northland.

Several suitable sailing dinghy designs in the 4m to 5m range are available, including some stock designs in fibreglass as well as older class racers like the Z-class and its near sister, the *Idle Along*. The main requirements for a safe and comfortable small cruiser are stability, ample buoyancy and stowage and, in the steep chop frequently found in shallow inshore waters where the wind and tide may work against each other, a dry boat is essential.

Our cruise is modest but the planning of *Tawaki*'s owner, Tony Scott, is a model for any dinghy cruise. Our course from Shelly Beach to Pahi, at the head of the Arapaoa River, near Paparoa, is carefully plotted on a topographical map. Sailing times for the three legs planned for the 55.5km journey are estimated on past experience with the boat and the likely effect of the tide.

Gear, carefully stowed in waterproof bags, includes flares and a first-aid kit. Crucial spares, tools and a knife are lashed within easy reach. An American writer offers this apt advice: 'Try thinking of the boat as a giant pack frame; gear developed for mountaineers can serve the open boat cruiser well.' The wide side decks and deep forepeak on *Tawaki* provide plenty of space for stowage. Generous splash boards and cockpit coaming ensure that bulky sleeping equipment that has been lashed around the centre case remains dry.

At 9am, with a detailed sailing plan in the hands of respective spouses and 40 minutes to high tide, we push off from Shelly Beach. Within 50m of the shore it is obvious that away from the protection of the beach the gentle south-westerly is really a determined blow. At 3.8m the Z-class is near the bottom of the suitable size range but its stability cannot be faulted as the mainsail is dropped at sea.

We are probably overcautious sailing under jib alone, but we prefer not to take unwarranted risks, particularly with a design that has a reputation for burying its nose when overpowered running or reaching. Anyway, with the tide now in our favour we clip along on schedule – and can pour our coffee without spilling a drop. As the bluffs of South Head move closer we hug the shore and, mindful of the huge volume of water ripping out of the harbour entrance, sneak around the head.

We lunch ashore and wait for the tide to turn. Three hours later we cast off for Tinopai, the tide now rushing back to help us on a relaxing broad reach under reefed main. The tide is still on the make when we reach our campsite on a deserted beach opposite Tinopai. We have no inflatable rollers so Tawaki is left at anchor while we carry our gear ashore. On a solo voyage she would probably be big enough to sleep on board under a boom tent. We opt for the comfort of a tent fly on the foreshore and a roaring driftwood campfire.

An early start, to catch the crucial tidal flow in the narrow confines to come, sees us away in thick fog. Only splashing mullet disturb the smoothness of the water, but we make good way, navigating by the hint of sun that is trying to melt away the fog. When it finally succeeds we are on course, through

adventure log

GETTING THERE: Put in at Shelly Beach on the South Head Road, past Helensville. Exit at Pahi, near Paparoa.

SAILING TIME: As long as you like but it can hardly be called a cruise if you don't overnight.

MAP: LINZ Q08, Q09, Q10.

FURTHER INFORMATION: See DINGHY CRUISING: THE ENJOYMENT OF WANDERING AFLOAT by Margaret Dye. Also read SEA KAYAKING: THE ESSENTIAL GUIDE TO EQUIPMENT AND TECHNIQUES by Johan Loots for good advice equally applicable to sailing dinghies.

The stillness persists as we tenaciously claw our way towards Pahi as the tide turns. Estuary sailing requires chess-like concentration. A lone pine on a headland can alter the wind direction sufficiently to force a tack. With only a gentle breeze to help us fight the tide it seems we might have to anchor and wait for it to return in our favour.

But taking advantage of the eddies inside bends, and by creeping up the shallow water on the edge of the estuary, we finally manage to cheat the tidal flow. As we lash the *Tawaki* on to her trailer for the journey home, our thoughts are as much on the cruises to come and the bays to be explored, as the shakedown so successfully completed.

the tour de kaipara

Bicycle, bicycle. I want to ride my bicycle, I want to ride my bike. Queen's lyrics are haunting me. Freddie Mercury wrote 'Bicycle Race' in 1978 after watching the Tour de France pass his hotel. I'm not into racing, I just want to ride my bike. But where?

I consult the Kennett brothers' *Classic New Zealand Mountain Bike Rides* but the only rides reasonably close to hand are in the Riverhead and Woodhill Forests and they are not really what I want. Keen mountain-bikers at Riverhead tend to be just that. They love to cycle up and down tracks – preferably down – for a couple of hours of sweaty, muddy recreation, throw their bikes back on the car rack and drive home.

Great fun but I want a day-long adventure and those the Kennetts list are too far away. So with inspiration from the Kennett boys I consult a map of the Woodhill Forest and the South Head of the Kaipara Harbour. A day-long bicycle adventure stares out. Lake Ototoa near the end of the strip of land that encloses the southern reaches of the Kaipara Harbour is the closest trout fishery to metropolitan Auckland, a delightful spot. The Papakanui Spit and the sand hills facing the open sea are favoured areas for fishers who reach these remote spots by four-wheel-drive vehicle. Behind them is the Woodhill Forest, planted by the taxpayer to stabilise the dunes and since sold to private enterprise to stabilise the economy.

The lake seems a good place to start our ride because trout fishers park there and our cars should be safe. There are two cars at the entrance to the walkway that leads to the lake when we arrive at about 8am. We have an assortment of mountain-bikes, my cross bike – a sort of hybrid – and Chris with his road touring bike. It is not an ideal machine for this adventure but then Chris has pedalled it from one side of the United States to the other and around much of New Zealand.

South Head Road turns to loose gravel at Lake Ototoa but it is easy pedalling through rolling farmland and with an almost total absence of traffic.

GETTING THERE: Take South Head Road, past Helensville.

PEDALLING TIME: A nice day out.

MAP: LINZ Q09.

FURTHER INFORMATION: This trip should only be attempted at dead low tide; it can be dangerous otherwise. For more inspiration consult CLASSIC NEW ZEALAND MOUNTAIN BIKE RIDES by Paul, Simon and Jonathan Kennett.

In fact, it is almost too easy until after about an hour on the road we reach a gate – which I hadn't noticed was marked on the map – and a sign indicating that from now on the road is through private property.

The Kaipara lies a couple of hundred metres below us and a public path leads down to the foreshore at Mosquito Bay. The path has been deeply eroded by rain but it is just negotiable by bike. Knowing how tidal the Kaipara is I figure it should be possible to ride along the foreshore all the way to South Head – so long as the tide is fully out. So we pedal on and carry our bikes on our shoulders over the rocks when we cannot.

Before we reach the head we come to a small gully that runs into the cliff and up onto the farm paddocks on the plateau above. There has been an old jetty and rail line here at some time. Perhaps years ago the farm loaded stock from here. We take a lunch break in total isolation yet within easy reach of the country's largest city.

From the cliff-top trig at South Head the view seems to go all the way to Dargaville. From this vantage point the harbour entrance seems quite narrow and its treachery is disguised. It's a great view but down on the foreshore we have to travel on soft sand that even the mountain-bikes find almost impossible to negotiate. Our path is repeatedly blocked by fallen trees or logs washed up onto the beach. We are forced to either lift our bicycles over the obstacles or get wet up to our waists. I don't think Freddie Mercury would want to ride his bicycle here.

At length we reach hard sand and a park where the four-wheel-drivers leave their vehicles. From now on we can happily ride our bicycles over the tracks the fishers have made along the Waionui Inlet until we reach a picnic area at the edge of the Woodhill Forest and the start of the gravel road.

There are several roads through the forest. We take Perham Road, which hugs the inlet foreshore until turning into Tasman Road and cycling up onto the peninsula ridge and out of the forest. A young farm dog decides to follow me and he is still with us a couple of kilometres later when we stop for a rest.

A group back from a fishing expedition spot their pooch and take him home in the boat they are towing.

It's literally downhill now to Lake Ototoa. We have ridden our bikes over some varied country, most of it deserted. I don't know about Freddie Mercury but I think the Kennett brothers would have liked the ride. Ring, ring. Ring, ring.

out of the rat race

In a world far removed from the bustle of today Izaak Walton, the acknowledged father of freshwater fishing, concluded that 'God never did make a more calm, quiet, innocent recreation than angling'.

Writing more than 300 years ago on the joy of fishing he noted: 'No life, my honest scholar, no life so happy and so pleasant, as the life of a well governed angler; for when the lawyer is swallowed up with business, and the statesman is preventing or contriving plots, then we sit on cowslip banks, hear the birds sing, and possess ourselves in as much quietness as these silent silver streams, which we now see glide so quietly by us.'

The problem for any envious businessman sitting in the 19th floor of a city office block listening to a fax machine sing is that unless there is a helicopter pad on the roof the cowslip banks are half a day's journey away, aren't they?

Well, no. More likely half an hour in the company car could see lawyers and statesmen join fishing scholars to angle for old Izaak's trouts. And 45 minutes could have them casting for wild river trout with a pedigree that precedes that of those famed fish in Rotorua and Taupo.

'Calm, quiet, and innocent recreation' is possible in six lakes and one river all within an hour's drive of downtown Auckland. Another half-hour and the fishing possibilities expand considerably with cowslip banks along the Kauaeranga River on the Coromandel Peninsula and the Waikato and Waihou River systems.

But if such locations are just too far away to duck out to between business meetings, Lake Pupuke on Auckland's North Shore is certainly not. The deep suburban lake has an honoured place in New Zealand trout fishing because in 1883 the Auckland Acclimatisation Society liberated fry in the lake from among the first three importations of rainbow trout. And it was from healthy and vigorous 4kg hens netted from Pupuke that rainbow stock were bred and first released in the Rotorua lakes 10 years later.

The fishing from Pupuke's cowslip banks is not quite as 'excellent' or the fish as 'abundant' as the society reported in the 1892 season. But it continues to be stocked every year with large-growing strains of rainbow and brown yearlings from Lake Waikaremoana, and the water quality is constantly improving. A canoeist out doing early-morning training claims to have seen rainbow trout up to 2.5kg around the hospital jetty.

But the lake fishing near Auckland that is most likely to cause office workers and statesmen to slip out of the office on a quiet afternoon is at Ototoa, north of Helensville on the South Head of the Kaipara. So that is exactly what I did when I managed to persuade Johan Giacon, a doyen of Auckland's freshwater angling fraternity, to guide me on an Ototoa trip.

Giacon, whose Italian grandfather came to New Zealand to dig the Orakei railway tunnel, remembers with a chuckle the first trout he caught from a river bank. It was in the famed Waitahanui River at Lake Taupo, which a former editor of the *Herald* the late Budge Hintz, had made his personal stamping ground.

As Giacon hooked his first fish his wife was away picking blackberries using his newly purchased landing net to push the bushes aside. The leader on his line was too long and badly tied so it wouldn't run through his rod. As Giacon yelled for his wife to bring the net, Hintz strode up and declared that 'only Poms use nets'. Then he offered to help, ran his hand down the leader and with a couple of flicks released the fish.

When Giacon protested that Hintz had done it deliberately he was told: 'You didn't deserve it anyway.'

Now there can't be anything worth knowing about trout fishing that Giacon doesn't know – he is a life member and former president of Trout Unlimited, which gives voluntary labour to improve the environment of lakes and streams – nor can there be any fish he doesn't deserve.

Lake Ototoa is a Trout Unlimited project and members have constructed a metalled access path to protect a grove of kanuka trees. On the way there we stop to collect Peter Storey, a Trout Unlimited project director. Storey is excited about future prospects because strains of trout that are now being bred with fast-growth characteristics promise to improve the fishing at put-and-take fisheries like the lakes near Auckland. At Lake Ototoa the new releases are now accounting for fish of up to 2.5kg.

Storey is also enthusiastic about the future of the Wairoa River, the closest trout river to Auckland city, with 5km of fishing water over a wadeable shingle bed. He has caught fish up to 1.5kg that confirm the river is now a self-sustaining 'wild' fishery with fish spawning above and below the Hunua Falls.

With neither streams nor gravel beaches, Lake Ototoa has no places for trout to spawn – and on a weekday it is anything but wild. There is a slight wind to ruffle the gin-clear water as Giacon, Storey and I begin casting from the shore but nothing else ruffles our recreation. There are freshwater mussels on the bottom and shoals of inanga mill about my waders.

Giacon's advice is to take some shelter behind reed beds and cast out on an angle as if river fishing, mending the line in slowly. I move around the shore with the sun on my back, fly line flicking lazily across the water. It is quiet – but then old Izaak Walton also said that there was more to fishing than simply catching fish.

I promise myself three more casts. On the second I have a powerful take on the line that bends the rod double but the fish is not hooked. Storey has similarly had no luck while Giacon has caught and released a young fish. But the point has been made. The calm, quiet, innocent recreation that God made is just a wing and a prayer from downtown Auckland.

Perhaps the only difference from Walton's day is that a licence is now required and there are various restrictions on fish size and numbers.

But then any artist would approve of that.

Paddling into the wilderness on the Hoteo River, between Wellsford and the Kaipara Harbour.

A flying start to a family rafting adventure on the upper Mohaka River, not far from Taupo.

A classic event around the Cavalli Islands in a Puffin-design sea kayak bought with money saved from kicking the habit. (Malcolm Pulman)

Lake Rotoaira, Pihanga and Lake Taupo appear as the snow runs out on a winter journey over the Tongariro Crossing.

When the going gets tough the tough keep going on a cycle circumnavigation of the South Head of the Kaipara Harbour.

where no man has gone before

Whakapapa ski school instructor Craig Corbett bears just the faintest resemblance to Captain Kirk but his briefing comes straight from the bridge of the *Enterprise*. 'This week you are to go where no man has gone before,' he says – or at least something to that effect. 'You will seek out ice, slush, deep untracked porridge, patches of cannonball-sized ice and hectares of soft powder. You will explore the steepest of slopes, plunge into unknown terrain. And when you return you will ski with confidence and fluidity over whatever obstacle a ski field may present.'

It is hard to take notes with ski gloves on but that, anyway, is the gist of Corbett's introduction to 8 hours of ski instruction I badly need. My trouble is that all the ski time and lesson money I have invested in my children has begun to pay off – I can barely keep up with them.

So I join six other oldies with the personable 'Captain Craig'. He tells us that for the next two days we are going to ski all those places we normally avoid – the other 300ha of this 400ha ski field. They are places away from the groomed trails, often deserted but often with the best snow and most interesting terrain.

It sounds freaky but Corbett reassuringly says that people of 'our ability' – hear that, kids? – can easily handle it. At our level, he says, it only takes some subtle changes of technique, barely noticeable to an untrained observer, to ski through ice, powder and soft snow on the one run without losing any rhythm.

For 8 solid hours he proceeds to show us how. He does so by a clever progression of ski experiences that helps us to 'feel' what we are doing: 'Don't over-analyse it,' he cautions. We ski on our toes to see what that does to a turn. Then on our heels. Then with pressure on our toes at the beginning of a turn and on our heels at the end.

It perhaps sounds technical but Corbett then leads us off onto a run that forces us to focus on what we have just been shown. Oh, so that's why I did that on the ice, we think to ourselves. Now if I do it deliberately it won't be scary and I can maintain a rhythm.

By the end of the second day and another 4 hours of going where I have never been before, I am ready to show off to the kids. They have been raving about their lessons – he, it seems, because of the jumps he is taken over and she because her instructor is so groovy. There must have been more to it than that because I am still having difficulty following my son to a jump he wants to show me and instead of having to wait for my daughter she is hot on our heels.

The real reward for going back to ski school becomes apparent a week later. It is one of those miserable days at Mt Ruapehu when I am usually the first off the ski field – except it is a weekday and there seem to be few people here. And Craig Corbett said our mission was to seek out the crud, to go looking for the places where we would not normally ski.

So we head for the upper mountain where big, wet snowflakes are falling and I can just pick out two other skiers on the Waterfall T-bar. The liftie is hiding in his hut and who can blame him.

But hey, this is fun. Pull your head forward, Corbett said, and I grab my hair like he did. Stand a little more aggressively, hands and knees prepared for the unknown. A red marker pole comes out of the murk. Yahoo. Soft snow, patch of ice, it's all the same to me. And for once it's the kids who give in first.

A day later when there is a window of sunshine between two fronts the rained-on snow has turned to bullet-proof ice. No problems. The noise of ski edges sliding and biting is horrific but there is no sound of heart-thumping. Nothing to it when you have already been to the outer limits of subtle pressures and edge sets. Even son makes clucking noises of approval – and then heads for the café to wait for the snow to soften.

The final test is on one of the guided trips the Whakapapa ski patrol runs each day. Five of us head off with Ken, who says, 'That's enough talk, let's ski.' We take the Traverse of Fear and ski down to the West Ridge quad chairlift. My companions seem to turn as effortlessly as Corbett, but I am holding my own and pleased with myself for being able to.

We take the Far West T-bar and go down Wizards, a delightful ridge trail that not many ski. Now the ice turns into soft snow, almost porridge, as we drop down the Amphitheatre, traverse and then head down Angus' Face. I have never skied some of these trails. There are huge Sunday crowds here – somewhere. That's the idea of the guiding service, says Ken. To show you other parts of the ski field.

We cross the top of Tennent's Valley, ski over the Rock Garden, and drop into a deserted valley to the top of Meads Wall. The beginners on the rope-tows must wonder what is happening as we carefully ski past them to the small chairlift that will take us out of the Happy Valley beginners' area.

I haven't time to tell them I'm just following orders. I have gone from the top of the mountain to the bottom, to a place where I have never gone before.

seven summits in seven hours

At 196m above the waters of the Waitemata Harbour, the summit of Mt Eden is a good deal lower than the 4897m-high bulk of Vinson Massif, highest mountain in Antarctica. On a sunny autumn day it is also considerably warmer. And with two coach-loads of tourists at the summit car park and dozens of Aucklanders out enjoying a fine day, it is also a lot more crowded.

But as I swig from a water bottle and enjoy with Joe Scott-Woods, my climbing partner, the panoramic view of what I consider to be the best-looking city in the world, I cast a thought towards Vinson. It's one reason why I'm sitting on Mt Eden. Back in 1990 the late Gary Ball and Rob Hall climbed the Antarctic peak with just a few hours to spare in their quest to climb the seven highest summits on the seven continents of the world within seven months. Ball's philosophy of adventure was one I endorse. He shunned elitism and competition, it was just 'being out there' that mattered. Ball admired an adventure no matter how modest: what it achieved was relative only to where it began. Everyone had their own Everest. He would have appreciated our little urban adventure. We have climbed seven summits in as many hours. We conceived our eccentric urban adventure as an alternative to braving what was forecast to be a windswept harbour.

Predictably it is a still and hot day as we tackle our first summit, Mt Albert, up a right-of-way where there was once a tramline that carried scoria down from the quarry.

Mt Albert was one of the first of Auckland's 48 volcanoes to emerge. It erupted more than 30,000 years ago when New Zealand was in the grip of the last ice age and the region consisted of two wide river valleys, the Manukau and Waitemata, separated by a low divide. The explosion left a crater about 300m across rimmed by a 60m-high rubble pile. Within hours molten rock oozed out of the crater and flowed down stream-beds towards Pt Chevalier and Western Springs. Stand on the Mt Albert summit now and you can still follow the line of lava flow.

To the east is Mt Albert's neighbour, Mt Roskill, a dumpy 109m volcano that has been little affected by quarrying. Today the two peaks are virtually joined by a wide green belt that runs beside Stoddard Road, and our feet barely need touch pavement.

East again is the Big King, last of the Three Kings that were born about 15,000 years ago in the most violent explosion of all the Auckland volcanoes. If it occurred today it would shatter every window in central Auckland. The eruption spewed huge quantities of ash and tuff over a wide area, including the neighbouring cones of Mt St John, One Tree Hill and Mt Hobson.

It initially left a crater about 300m deep that filled with lava and solidified, formed three cones and sent lava flowing about 10km to the Waitemata River to become Tetokaroa Reef. The extent of quarrying that has left just one 139m cone intact is clear when you climb to the water tower on the summit. Not much of the volcano is left but there is a vast space around it, suitable perhaps for a future amphitheatre.

One Tree Hill dominates the skyline to the east, even though its single tree is sadly missing from the 183m summit. But at least the volcano, given to the city by Sir John Logan Campbell, has been saved from the ravages inflicted on the Three Kings.

We stop for lunch at a pavement café at Greenwoods Corner where the waitress eyes our water bottles and daypacks and asks what country we are from. Perhaps only mad dogs and tourists go mountain climbing in the autumn sun.

Unlike most of the other volcanoes One Tree Hill (Maungakiekie) erupted several times, beginning about 18,000 years ago. An estimated half a cubic kilometre of lava flowed from several vents to leave a lava bed 60m to 80m thick reaching to the edge of the Auckland Domain and south almost to the Manukau Harbour.

We climb through a grove of huge olive trees. The summit of Maungakiekie, stronghold of the 18th-century ruler of the area, Kiwi Tamaki, is a commanding spot. Its extensive terracing and numerous storage pits are evidence of the thousands of people who lived here until they were driven out by intertribal warfare in the late 18th century. Auckland is blessed with this park and many of its citizens are out enjoying it. Some drive to admire the view, others walk and many others picnic beneath the oak trees of Cornwall Park.

We cross Greenlane Road, walk past the back of the showgrounds to Market Road and the smallest of our summits, Mt St John, its height considered too insignificant to be given on the Auckland topographical map. Yet surprisingly when you get to the top there is a large crater for the residents in the area to play in – and those olive trees again.

Its near neighbour, Mt Hobson, on the other side of the Southern Motorway, is considerably larger. Stiles along the backyard fenceline suggest that residents don't take the park for granted. There are also some apples hanging over the fence, welcome fuel for a couple of tiring mountaineers.

Mt Hobson's western flank has been considerably modified to accommodate a huge water reservoir but the northern flank is touched only by graffiti drawn on the grass for the benefit of motorway users. To the north-east is a delightful view of the Orakei waterfront that is otherwise exclusive to a couple of large houses.

Six down and one to go. Across Newmarket, past Government House and a direct assault on the east face of Mt Eden. We top the face where a young couple are picnicking under a tree, and follow the ridge to the summit with time to spare before our 7 hours are up.

classic weekend at mahurangi

A flash of parochial pride is unavoidable as the ferry passenger, in thick German accent, exclaims: 'This is why they call it the City of Sails.'

His companion is training a video camera on the Friday-night fleet heading out of the Waitemata for a long weekend in the near and distant reaches of the Hauraki Gulf.

'If you think that is something, wait until Monday,' I mutter to no one in particular.

Monday is Auckland's Anniversary Day and that has always been synonymous with sailing. It was once the day for reputedly the largest one-day regatta in the world. As a cadet reporter I would sit at a long table in the Tamaki Yacht Club typing endless lists of race results to be printed in the following day's *New Zealand Herald*. There were tiny P-class yachts, and A-class giants with classic names like *Ranger, Moana, Rawhiti, Ngataringa, Prize, Little Jim*, and the wonderful gaff-rigged *Ariki*. Close-hauled or downwind to Kawau, the handsome fleet regularly graced the pages of the old *Weekly News* and you didn't have to be a yachting buff, or a cadet reporter, to know that *Ranger* was the Cardigan Bay of the Waitemata.

I eventually got into the thick of Anniversary Day regattas sitting in the bilge of a naval whaler and bailing for a couple of hours. It might not sound like much fun but it was probably one of the best ways to 'feel' a city sailing because the leaden whalers were always among the first fleets to start and the last to finish. As we crawled our way up and down the harbour, modern yachts, in endless variety, would sail past. My fellow ferry passenger with his video camera would have run out of tape long before we got the finishing gun.

The navy has retired its whalers and the Anniversary Day regatta on the Waitemata is no longer the blitz of sail it used to be. There are a lot of other attractions on a holiday weekend. But the tradition remains, on the Waitemata and elsewhere, which is why I am on the Devonport ferry.

The regatta on the Waitemata Harbour might be better known, but just up the coast at Mahurangi an Anniversary Weekend regatta was born in 1858 out of rivalry between the pioneering Sullivan and Jackson families. Within two years the series of family rowing and sailing races had become a fully-fledged regatta. It continued, somewhat sporadically, for decades until lapsing during the Second World War.

In 1977 the Friends of Mahurangi, a group originally formed to oppose the disposal of sewage into the harbour, revived it. Mahurangi is an appropriate spot at which to celebrate the region's maritime heritage. Out of its reaches came some of the early craft on which trade in the north depended for decades. A Mahurangi-built cutter was launched in 1849 and with it the birth of a shipbuilding industry using the kauri of the hinterland.

Some of the Mahurangi timber may well be in the A-class classic *Moana*, built in Auckland in 1895 by the famous Logan Brothers, John and Robert junior, to lines drawn by Arch Logan, and pride of the Hauraki Gulf and Waitemata Harbour racing fleet ever since. *Moana*, A9, is typical of her day at 14.3m long overall and a water-line length of 9.9m. Her 2.7m beam is wide for the period and her powerful hull is capable of carrying a large sail area.

The big keeler sits spic and span on her mooring near Devonport wharf. Her skipper Chris Smith, rows in to pick me up. We have over half an hour to make the start line off Devonport wharf for the annual night race to Mahurangi. It is a privilege to be given the opportunity to crew on such a craft. The experience goes far beyond mere nostalgia. *Moana* epitomises not so much an age but a belief that simplicity, honesty and hard work really matter.

It is in the nature of these old thoroughbreds to turn most voyages into a race, and getting to Mahurangi for a weekend of fun is no exception. It gets dark before we reach Whangaparaoa. Fireworks on the horizon from an international athletics meeting are no match for the panoply of stars overhead. At sea level the only lights are the pinprick navigation lights of other yachts.

We do quite well with only *Rawhiti* ahead of us as we sail through the Tiri Passage. Night sailing carries a wonderful sense of speed that is not always justified. Somewhere out of the darkness behind us the fleet picks up a breeze that *Moana*, closer in shore, misses. As we close on the finish we hear *Prize* and *Little Jim* call out their names. *Ngataringa* and *Rawhiti* are already home.

Bleary eyes in the morning adjust to a romantic sight. The whole of Otarawao (formerly Sullivans Bay) is filled with yachts at anchor, including the majestic *Breeze* moored near us. Puttering between the vintage yachts is a small steamboat that gives a good-morning toot on its whistle.

They knew how to enjoy themselves at old-time regattas and at Mahurangi they recapture that spirit of family fun. On the beach there are egg-and-spoon, sack and three-legged races, lolly scrambles, sand sculpturing and a tug-of-war. There are rowing and running races for every age group – and there is the Mahurangi Cup, the major race for wooden boats of pre-1955 design.

adventure log

GETTING THERE: The turn-off to the Auckland regional park at Mahurangi West is off SH 1 just past Puhoi.

BE INSPIRED: The park is one of the region's gems with many opportunities for walking, kayaking and camping.

FURTHER INFORMATION: ARC info from ParksLine 0-9-303 1530. To crew on a classic yacht contact Classic Yacht Association of New Zealand 0-9-413 9406.

This is serious stuff. *Moana* is short-handed but Smith is going to fly his Yankee anyway and we round Saddle Island behind *Rawhiti* and *Ngataringa*. Smith barks commands to ease or tighten the staysail or jib. Up and down go the foresails, in and out go the sheets. It is hard work. Tomorrow my shoulder muscles and hands will feel the effects.

We are comfortably holding our position in the fleet. Third across the line and some compensation for our effort the previous night. You are entitled to enjoy a gin and tonic with a slice of lemon after a race like that. It seems the right drink on a classic yacht.

around the whirl in 50km

Some people have all the luck. After yet another weekend of rain the sky clears and the sun comes out on Monday. Along the Auckland waterfront a handful of people cock a snook at work routines to take advantage of the pale winter sunshine. At Okahu Bay two women picnic on the beach while their babies sleep peacefully on a blanket. On the Tamaki Drive footpath and cycle track are fitness walkers, elderly people out for a stroll and tourists breathing in the Waitemata Harbour and islands of the inner Hauraki Gulf.

It is the sort of time and place when it feels good to be alive and smug that you have planned this day to bypass the office and cycle around the Auckland isthmus on a 50km tour route promoted by the Auckland Regional Council, the Auckland Cycle Touring Association and the Auckland City Council.

The route starts in the Auckland Domain, swings past the Parnell Rose Gardens and on to Tamaki Drive. In December the track will be paved with pohutukawa blossoms but today it is surrounded by the crispness of winter that seems to bring the view into sharper focus. Listless yachts at their moorings, the sun reflecting off a calm sea and only a seagull to break the silence. Well, that's not quite true. Trucks and buses rumble by but they make little impression on the picture postcard I cycle through.

At Mission Bay where summer riders might stop for a swim, I pause for lunch at a pavement café and discover the best hamburger that I have ever tasted. The enormous black-pepper burger from Thunderburgers lies a little heavily on the steep climb out of St Heliers to Achilles Point.

I follow the blue route signs, which are strategically placed on lamp posts, into Riddell Road. Decades ago this was one of *the* Auckland streets. You don't hear so much about it now but the reasons for its stature remain – sunny clifftop views across the Waitemata Harbour to Browns Island, Motu-tapu and far beyond. The stock grazing on Churchill Park, a farm in the middle of suburbia, take no notice as I pedal past. Further on is the Tahuna Torea Reserve, a wading-bird sanctuary that if I had more time would have demanded a departure from my cycling plans.

Down into Glen Innes I am getting into familiar territory. As a youth I used to traipse through these state-house streets on a Saturday morning to collect money from subscribers to the *Herald*. They seem to have changed very little in the nearly 40 years since. Some homes are immaculately tended with neat lawns and trim gardens while others are depressing dumps of long grass, old cars and broken windows.

adventure log

GETTING THERE: You can join the 50km cycle anywhere on the route but somewhere on the Auckland waterfront where you can park your car is a good choice.

PEDALLING TIME: About half a day, but why not stop for lunch or a latte and make a leisurely journey of it.

MAP: Any Auckland street map will do.

FURTHER INFORMATION: The route is well sign-posted. If in doubt contact Auckland City Council 0-9-379 2020.

It's brighter down Riverside Avenue, where state-house tenants used to gaze across the Tamaki River at a mirror image of the view commanded by the expensive real estate on the eastern shore. Now some of the old state houses are advertised for auction with 'views forever'.

At the bottom of Kings Road in Panmure are the grounds of the Tamaki Rugby Club and the St George's Rowing Club shed. It was always dark when I used to cycle up this street after rugby training, or down it to rowing training. In winter, hands would be red from cold.

The street doesn't seem as long now, but at the top of it there is still part of an old hotel moved onto the site years ago and indelibly etched on my memory for the smell of fish-head soup that used to waft out of the back door whenever I called for the *Herald* money. Nearly opposite is a Fencibles stone cottage that was used by the caretaker at a factory my father managed and was moved, stone by stone, to the high-street site. The factory has gone, given way to McDonald's.

From Mt Wellington the cycle route goes to the Ellerslie racecourse and into Cornwall Park. What a treasure Sir John Logan Campbell bequeathed his city. I'd like to look at his old cottage but time is pressing so I cycle past the sheep in the One Tree Hill Domain and along a series of quiet, leafy back streets running parallel with Mt Albert Road.

I follow the route past the old elephant enclosure of Auckland Zoo and up Motions Road – for all of a couple of metres before giving in to the inevitable and pushing the bike. It should be called Slow Motions Road. Now it's almost all downhill to the Westhaven Marina and back to the Domain.

In 50km I have cycled past or through 20 major parks and numerous smaller reserves, around the foreshore of a harbour and past several sandy beaches. I have seen cattle and sheep grazing, some small patches of native bush, numerous birds, modern and historic homes and a pot pourri of city life.

Cavers are a happy bunch. Perhaps they need cheery dispositions, or to be slightly mad, to spend their recreation hours underground – but it is a particularly jovial crew I meet in the rain outside a Waipu dairy.

I am here at the invitation of Kevin Jose and Quenton Foreman of the Auckland Speleological Group. Both are also alpinists, back-country skiers, trampers and sea kayakers but rarely on any of those exploits have I encountered the sort of cohesive, good-natured ambience that seems to exist among the bunch of cavers I have joined.

Maybe the close proximity of their environment has something to do with it. Maybe it's the shared experience of standing in the rain on the side of the road in the middle of nowhere, stripping off and pulling on a wetsuit and a strange assortment of gumboots, old overalls, hard hats and rubber dishwashing gloves.

I am not feeling quite as cheerful as those around me. I'm a bit apprehensive about what I have let myself in for. The bunch with which I am squelching across a muddy paddock in the rain has been underground a lot more than once. The battered clothing is a giveaway. So is the eagerness on their faces as they purposely walk towards a huge, bush-covered limestone hill.

We reach the bush and a stream that disappears into a tiny opening in the base of the hill. One after the other, we crouch down and, like a leaf tossed into the stream, follow it through the opening.

The first impression is one of pleasant surprise. I had imagined that the candle-sized flame of our carbide lamps would give a flickering, eerie light. Instead, the combined glow of eight lamps lights up the cave like an average-sized electric light bulb. I could easily read a book – if I was not slithering on my stomach through the centre of the stream, using my elbows for propulsion.

It is soon evident how Two Tone got its name. The stream is eating into a solid greywacke base that rises a little up the sides of the passage. Above that is the creamy hue of limestone. It falls in folds, with stalactite spears and assorted sculptures that defy imagination. The bright sparkling of glow-worms adds a final magical quality.

We reach a chamber where the limestone has been left like pools of water. Above there is a vast assortment of crystals and stalactites, some as thick as a fence post and others as delicate as a straw.

I discover with some relief that keeping a secure footing is not a problem. The limestone underfoot is like sandpaper – hence the dishwashing gloves – and there is no fear of feet slipping. Where to put one's hard-hatted head is more of a problem. Turn carelessly and a helmet could smash the fragile beauty of the cave as easily as a sledgehammer.

Fortunately cavers seem the most conservation-minded of all outdoor pursuiters. Jose tells me that if this stalactite-studded cavern had just been discovered it would be roped off to ensure that no one could accidentally damage the beauty that has taken thousands of years to form. Cavers are also imaginative. We have been traversing Udder Passage, named after limestone formations that bear a strong resemblance to a certain part of a cow's anatomy.

We reach two 4m-high waterfalls. A length of climbing tape is tied off above the waterfall and, with the tape under our shoulders and around our backs as a brake, we abseil down the falls. It reminds me of Jose explaining that caves are an easy environment to get into but difficult to rescue someone out of. Despite that, caving is relatively accident-free because most people have the sense to go underground with experienced companions.

The cave survey map says 'swim' and that is exactly what we have to do to negotiate two deep pools. One by one our heads go bobbing along the stream with our carbide lamps glowing.

We have entered the cave system by a side stream and when we reach the main stream we stop for lunch. Then we head up the Duck Waddle, where the cave roof is too low to walk bent over and too high to warrant stomach slithering. I watch Jose in front of me. He squats and, with both arms extended behind him for balance, he disappears out of sight. He is going so fast that he looks more like a crab than a waddling duck.

My legs are not up to waddling and I have to settle for crawling on my hands and knees. The duck sections are the most uncomfortable part of the trip and my knees protest at the stony stream-bed. There are a couple of 3m waterfalls to climb before we head for an entrance called Irresistible Daylight Duck. It is so named because the last metre or two has to be negotiated submerged in the stream but no one, I am told, minds putting their head under because the light of the cave entrance shines through irresistibly.

The water level of the stream, which is a little swollen by recent rain, gets higher and the roof of the cave lower. When they meet we are still some way off Irresistible Daylight Duck, so we retrace our steps and head out the Escape Route. It is an old passage covered in mud and flood debris. It provides an interesting contrast to some of the passages we have been

adventure log

GETTING THERE: The Waipu Caves complex is near Waipu between Maungaturoto and Whangarei.

TIME UNDERGROUND: Most caving trips are for less than a day but in some of the more extensive systems cavers may spend a night or longer underground.

FURTHER INFORMATION: Caving is not a DIY sport. Contact Auckland Speleo Group 0-9-627 4260, www.asg.org.nz.

through and helps to explain what cavers mean when they talk about good caves and bad caves.

Jose, who started caving through a tramping club trip and has been hooked on it since, feels there is something almost spiritual about caves. The power of nature evident in a cave and the enormous timescale that its formation represents is humbling.

When we reach daylight we have been underground for $4^1/_4$ hours. The bush smells refreshing. I am allowed to feel a little relieved because the cavers tell me they always feel a buzz when they emerge from a cave; a sort of feeling of satisfaction.

gently does it on the barrier

Four days on Great Barrier Island gives a whole new meaning to the notion of a 'gently undulating track'. That is the comforting description given the route for the first morning of a Hillary Commission Big Coast cycling event. But the 150 riders in this non-competitive mountain-bike trek soon discover as they cycle through Great Barrier Forest Park that 'gentle' is a relative word on a rocky and mountainous island.

By the time the first morning is over it is beginning to feel like the route has been chosen by the Grand Old Duke of York. Dedicated mountain-bikers live for downhills that they attack at kamikaze speeds. A hill is only a means to another downhill. The rest of us enjoy downhills too because it's a chance to get a bit of air into bursting lungs. But our enjoyment is tempered by the sure knowledge that when we are down we are not going to be staying there with the Duke of York's 10,000 men. On Great Barrier a downhill is just a prelude to another uphill.

Yet the beauty of this event is that downhill bombers and uphill sloggers can ride pretty much together for four days, enjoy the journey and each other's company and not give a hoot about who rides into camp first and who pedals in last. And after four days undulating in that sort of company even the ramparts of the Barrier start to seem a little gentle.

We begin in darkness at Whangaparapara Harbour. It says something for the fortitude of these outdoor eventers that they should ride a kilometre then pitch a tent under the light of the Milky Way and, after hot chocolate and cake from the Awana Women's Division of Federated Farmers, nod off to sleep without the merest hint of mayhem. It's as well to pass that little test in outdoor skills because on the morrow we face 16km of gentle undulations.

It's actually not too tough at all, just a bit of a shock to an untrained body. What is more of a shock is the way this rugged landscape has been savagely modified by the timber-milling vandals of last century. No battlement or narrow gorge escaped their axes and saws as they stripped kauri from the land. Worse still were the fires that the bushmen, gumdiggers and farmers deliberately lit to lay waste to the land.

The forest park is one of the few places where the bush has begun to regenerate without being knocked back by successive fires. The big kauri have mostly gone but there is no shortage of solid, healthy kauri rickers. Down near the mouth of the Kaiarara Stream, where the Kauri Timber Company flushed an estimated 90 million feet of timber, is a kauri planted in 1953. Its size is certainly promising.

adventure log

GETTING THERE: By Fullers Auckland ferry from the Auckland downtown ferry terminal.

RIDING TIME: You could go to the Barrier for a weekend but you need a 4- to 5-day trip – whether for tramping, cycling or sea kayaking – to get the best out of the island.

MAP: Great Barrier Island Infomap 336-02.

FURTHER INFORMATION: DOC information brochures. DOC Auckland 0-9-379 6467; DOC Great Barrier 0-9-429 0044; visitor information 0-9-429 0033; Fullers Auckland 0-9-367 9111. Read GREAT BARRIER ISLAND by Don Armitage.

Under the stewardship of the New Zealand Forest Service thousands of seedling kauri, totara, rimu and the like were planted, explains DOC ranger Stan McGeady, who was born and bred in Whangaparapara from where the largest timber mill in the Southern Hemisphere once exported direct to Europe. The mill has been gone since the 1920s. Now young backpacking visitors like Peter and Martine from Belgium enjoy the solitude in DOC's delightful Whangaparapara campsite.

We take a small break from our bikes to scale the rocky heights of Maungapiko. All around is an extensive and tempting network of tramping tracks. At Port Fitzroy we enjoy a hearty lunch from the fund-raising mothers of Okiwi school before cycling up and over the island to beautiful, deserted Whangapoua Beach, where any aches after a day in the saddle are soon washed away in the sea.

The Maby family, whose hospitality we enjoy, have farmed here since 1910. In their backyard are orange trees seeded from fruit that washed ashore when the steamer *Wairarapa* sank off the Barrier in 1894. At the end of the beach are the graves of some of the 121 people who died. There are also rocks that mountain-bike trekkers snorkel around and catch fish from before tucking into hangi food prepared by the Motairehe Marae.

There is a lot to be said for these catered-and-carried treks. Julie and Lance Mexted and Peter Robinson relax on deckchairs in front of the large frame tent they have brought from Pauatahanui, near Wellington.

'I'd still be sitting on my backside smoking forty cigarettes a day if a friend hadn't persuaded me to go in the Wellington Big Coast a couple of years ago,' says Julie. 'I had to get fit for that ride and I have just kept at it.'

Next morning, under the curious gaze of a flock of rare brown teal whose backyard our tent city has temporarily shared, we point our front wheels towards Harataonga Bay and the Great Divide. That is actually the polite word for this hill climb, which winds its way from sea level to about 350m. The locals have much more colourful descriptions and have taken great delight in telling us about the trial we face.

They are incredulous that one rider should ascend in 16 minutes and full leg amputee Martin Clark pedal up comfortably with one leg – and then unstrap his crutches from his bike and take off to the 621m summit of Mt Hobson (Hirakimata). But many of us are happy to walk much of the way up the Great Divide and eternally grateful that Shirley Amos and her Okiwi School mothers are waiting at the top with drinks, watermelon and fresh muffins.

The walk into Windy Canyon, the track to Mt Hobson, is spectacular. A strong breeze rustles the foliage through narrow rock clefts that we ascend up steep wooden steps. About 40ha around Mt Hobson, highest point on the Barrier, is all that escaped the bushman's axe. Black petrels nest in burrows around the summit and we must be careful not to leave the track.

Great Barrier folk are alleged to claim Overtons Beach at Harataonga Bay as the best on the island. It is one of those idyllic east coast beaches, fringed with pohutukawa and rocky points and protected by an island, the Dragon, lying offshore. The DOC campsite, around a meandering stream, is superb. There are kayaks available to paddle out to the Island, pa sites to explore and rocks to fish from. The gung-ho take their bikes to the top of a steep paddock and descend at blinding speed to the roar of a ready-made audience. The fastest clocks above 60 km/h. Dinner is an Irish stew cooked by the O'Shea family and supporters of the Taurehere Marae, a new group that hopes to build a multicultural community centre.

Day three and the 2.5km climb out of the bay goes more easily than we had dared even imagine when descending. The night's camp is at Medlands Beach.

On day four fat tyres are beginning to handle the Barrier's metal roads comfortably so we take an afternoon ride back to some hot springs that fringe the Kaitoke swamp. Rain can do nothing to dampen the huge spread that the

Tryphena Sports and Recreation Club put on for us. Nor can the drizzle deter last-night partying around a campfire with the locals.

It's a long steep hill out of Medlands but no one, from 85-year-old John Trotter to speedy 17-year-old Marvyn Joll, seems to notice these gentle undulations now.

Abel Tasman
National Park

Marlborough
Sounds

NELSON

Inland
Kaikoura
Range

GREYMOUTH

HOKITIKA

CHRISTCHURCH

Aoraki Mt Cook
National Park

QUEENSTOWN

Fiordland
National Park

DUNEDIN

INVERCARGILL

southern sojourns

Many consider that the mountains, river valleys and sounds of the South Island are the New Zealand outdoors. There is a grandeur in the southern island that cannot be ignored – so long as you have a few lifetimes to explore the opportunities.

the idyll of abel tasman

When they cut blocks of granite from Tonga Bay on the Abel Tasman coast to build Nelson Cathedral they left the altar on the beach. Grains of sand like no other lie along the bay and others of the Abel Tasman National Park. Quartz and marble eroded to a glistening honey-coloured sugar sparkles in the sunlight, a soft, beguiling border between the green hills of regenerating native bush and a turquoise sea of clearest water.

Other countries have beaches with white sands of talcum powder softness or the sugar of crushed coral but the sandy coves of Abel Tasman have a colour and texture that each year attracts the footprints of thousands of worshippers from around the world.

The smallest of New Zealand's national parks, 22,139ha tucked in to the north-west tip of the South Island, Abel Tasman has become a New Zealand icon, its image almost as instantly recognisable as Mt Taranaki or the All Black uniform. Its size is its first distinction. It has an intimacy that is reassuring, a promise of safety and an experience in the outdoors that is achievable, a challenge to the senses rather than the body. Its physical features are enigmatic. There is that golden sand and the crescent-shaped coves flanked by granite sculptures carved by nature. In places it evokes an image of the tropics and coral atolls – except that fur seals laze on the rocky foreshore.

Perhaps most importantly for the visitor, although most probably take it for granted, is that this national park, opened in 1942 after years of logging and slash-and-burn farming had denuded the hills, still contains remnants of private land and squatters' cottages that may remain for the owner's lifetime. That makes the park accessible to the old and young alike, to the fit and the almost infirm, because in the heart of the park there are luxury lodges where you can enjoy a gourmet meal and wallow in a comfy bed.

It means that the 38km coastal track from Marahau to Totaranui and a further 13km to Wainui Inlet, already the gentlest of the Department of Conservation's Great Walks, can be broken into easy chunks over a few days or even experienced as a day trip with any of a number of combinations of sightseeing by water taxi and perhaps a few hours of sea kayaking near the Tonga Island seal colony or a stroll along the coastal track – running shoes will do just fine – before being plucked from an idyllic cove by ferry.

Abel Tasman is a living park, a place where people and nature embrace. My embrace with the park begins in a sea kayak at Kaiteriteri Beach, just outside the national park boundary. Our guide Darryl spent his youth in urban Auckland where his most significant accomplishment was to sit next to Rachel Hunter in science class and spike her book with his compass when she annoyed him. Then he discovered the outdoors and now he wouldn't be anywhere else. Even Ms Hunter can't buy the paradise he works in.

He takes us close to features like Split Apple Rock to offer his version of a Maori legend as to why this huge granite boulder, surrounded by water, is neatly cleaved down the middle. We stop for lunch at Stream Cove on Adele Island, named by French explorer Dumont D'Urville after his wife. We have the sandy cove all to ourselves.

Between the island and the mainland is the Astrolabe Roadstead, a stretch of clear water named after D'Urville's ship, where a string of sandy bays and campsites are accessed from the coastal track. Torrent Bay has water access only and a clutch of holiday homes on a patch of private land. The lodge is at the water's edge. You can fish or swim or just laze around with a cold beer.

Next day the wind picks up and by lunchtime the weather has turned to rain. But the ever-resourceful Darryl plans our lunch break under the shelter of the Bark Bay Hut porch. Around the next point is the Tonga Island marine reserve, where taking any marine life is forbidden.

A tang of stale fish and urine in the wind is the first indication of the seal colony at Tonga Island. The seals have pups and lie well back in the rocks but one rolls on its back among our kayaks as though it is sick and cannot swim

adventure log

GETTING THERE: Adventures in Abel Tasman usually start in Motueka. Tour companies will pick you up in Nelson.

ADVENTURE TIME: Most people take 3 to 4 days, whether walking, kayaking, or a bit of both.

MAP: Abel Tasman Parkmap 273-07.

FURTHER INFORMATION: Abel Tasman is the country's most popular park and there is no shortage of information on it. Start with WALKING THE ABEL TASMAN COAST TRACK by Philip Holden; DOC park and track information brochures; DOC Motueka 0-3-528 0005. Abel Tasman National Park Enterprises 0800 223 582.

properly. It's cleaning itself, says Darryl, and as we watch it finally swims away just like a seal should.

At Onetahuti Beach we stash the kayaks above high water, from where they will be collected by a water taxi or a group travelling in the other direction, and don our shoes for a 40-minute walk over Tonga Saddle to Awaroa.

On day three we take a dinghy across the flooded Awaroa Inlet – you can walk at low tide – and follow the coast track around headlands where southern rata are in blazing glory, and along those magical Abel Tasman beaches to Totaranui and a road that takes you out of paradise.

a winner in the scenery stakes

It is the first Tuesday in November, a day when each year much of the country comes to a halt for about $3^1/_2$ minutes to watch a bunch of thoroughbreds gallop 3200m in pursuit of more than $2 million. Our gallop down the Queen Charlotte Track is over 67km and with no thoroughbreds among us it will take four days. But the rewards in sight seem worth so many millions that none of us remembers it is Melbourne Cup day.

Unending views are undoubtedly the prize for walking this long-distance trail in the Marlborough Sounds and they tend to leave little else to focus on. Around every bend in the undulating trail between Ship Cove and Anakiwa is yet another bush-framed view of distant hills, sparkling turquoise seas, a golden fringe of foreshore, idyllic bays and regenerating native bush. It prompts a litany of 'fantastics' from an English woman in our group, but any superlative seems inadequate for these big-screen images.

The track down the spine of land that separates Kenepuru Sound from Queen Charlotte Sound follows old bridle paths along the ridgeline. With the formation of the Marlborough Sounds Maritime Park, the old bridle trail was cleared of gorse to become one of the walkways in the national network. More recently, with other long-distance trails under tourist pressure, DOC upgraded the route so that it is suitable for mountain-bikes.

As wilderness walks go, they do not come much more forgiving than the Queen Charlotte Track. I am on a fully catered inn-to-inn trek. The ferry that takes us to Ship Cove, where Captain Cook spent 100 days between 1770 and 1771 repairing his ship and men, carries our luggage ahead for us each day – and for a small charge does so for independent walkers smart enough to carry nothing more than a daypack and water bottle.

Our guide, Kate Batten, is making her 41st trek along the trail and pampers us with knowledge and all our food and accommodation arrangements. For all that, it soon becomes obvious on the climb out of Ship Cove that no amount of nurturing will stop puffing and sweating along the trail.

Of this area Captain Cook wrote: 'The hills are one continual forest of lofty trees flourishing with a vigour almost superior to anything that imagination can conceive and affording an august prospect to those who are delighted with the grand and beautiful works of nature.' The sentiment did not stop Cook and those who followed from felling nature's works. Nonetheless, this is a reserve area and black beech has regenerated to lofty heights from which bellbird and tui follow our progress with a melodious chorus.

After a pleasant 5- to 6-hour walk we reach the head of Endeavour Inlet, where mussels are exposed on the foreshore at low tide and a wealthy Wellington merchant's holiday home from the late 19th century is now a comfortable lodge and tavern. We have time to carry on to Camp Bay and the luxurious Punga Cove resort, just 4 hours away on the other side of the inlet. But when you hurry in paradise you miss encounters with people such as Maria Buzzi, a jolly Italian octogenarian who early next morning at the end of Endeavour Inlet I find planting fruit trees.

The walkway runs through many stretches of private land and here there are wild foxgloves and lilies in the fields and a farmhouse with the jawbone of a wild pig nailed on almost every fence post. They are the work of Maria's husband, who when given the opportunity to leave his Italian hills, which the Allies were to give Tito, selected a photograph of green hills and the promise of wild pigs that Cook liberated in Queen Charlotte Sound in 1773. The Buzzis have no children but hundreds of walkers along the trail. 'I love to meet them,' Maria says in a lovably thick Italian accent. 'It gets lonely here.'

Out of Punga Cove on a 20km stretch to the Portage it can get wonderfully lonely too, because the trail climbs to over 470m with uphill stretches totalling about 1100m. Hills soon spread our group so that even on this trail it is possible to walk in contemplative isolation. The downhill section to Anakiwa is under a canopy of beech and rimu, accompanied by the trilling of birds, with glimpses of a cutter sailing on a turquoise lagoon – rewards indeed worth millions.

a climber's literary challenge

This story is not my idea; it never was. But mountain guides can be persuasive – they need to be to get clients up and down mountains. The late Gary Ball was a master of persuasion. When he suggested that so long as I am fit and determined he could take me to the top of Aoraki/Mt Cook, I was persuaded.

The challenge to climb New Zealand's highest mountain seems like a reasonable consolation prize for a middle-aged ego unlikely ever to be sated by wealth or promotion.

Ball gets me safely up the crevasse-riven Linda Glacier without being swatted by an ice avalanche crashing off Mt Vancouver. We crampon to the top of the Linda ice shelf before we must turn back in the face of a snow slope that he judges will avalanche. The next day it does while I take my aching muscles back to civilisation.

That should be the end of it except that muscular strains heal quicker than wounded pride and Ball's subsequent letters are full of ego-boosting reassurance. So two years later, after even more training, I am again on top of the ice shelf on Ball's rope.

The weather is perfect and so is the snow. And I'm feeling great. The trouble is that Ball, with 19 Cook summits under his boots, is not. He has been feeling sick and a bit dizzy for a couple of hours. It could be the flu, a touch of altitude sickness, a tummy bug or just stress from organising an expedition to Mt Everest that he is to embark on in a few days.

A couple of pitches (rope lengths) up the summit rocks we rest on the edge of the precipitous East Face, down which a few years later will slide millions of tonnes of rock and reduce the 3764m summit by 10m. Across the Tasman Glacier but now below us are the tips of the Liebig Range – and every other peak except Mt Tasman. Ball decides that he is not well enough to guide safely. He declares that we are going down. But first a photograph. It is hard to smile, although the result hangs on my office wall.

We try again a couple of days later but I quickly call it off; I am not fit enough and no longer focused. Nor am I satisfied. Ball says he'll put my deposit on the climb towards another attempt but with his international guiding career beginning to boom it gets as hard to pin him down as it is to find any friend or family member who thinks I am not suffering a serious mid-life crisis.

They have a point. There have to be better ways to spend a holiday than hanging around Mount Cook village waiting for the weather to clear, paying a fortune to get to a hut full of smelly, polypropylene-clad students, getting up at midnight only to find that weeks of pounding the Auckland pavements don't seem to have done much good, and then being defeated by the forces of nature.

The domestic dilemma is resolved when Japanese chef George Iwama survives a storm on Mt Ruapehu that claims six young lives. He is training, he says, for a climb of Mt Cook – a revelation that Mt Cook Group publicists cannot ignore. Nor is its subsequent all-expenses offer to Iwama something I can ignore. The offer begs publicity; I volunteer to provide it.

So after days of waiting in Mount Cook village for a weather change, and a night in an overcrowded and smelly hut, I again trudge up the Linda Glacier, this time with notebook and pencil in hand. Iwama and I both have guides and there are two others carrying television cameras. At the top of the Bowie Ridge we enlarge a bergschrund into a sizeable snow cave. In a tent near us is another guide, Guy Cotter, and an American client.

When we leave the snow cave at 2am there are no stars in the sky. The weather is ominous. We wait while Iwama and his guide take the first pitch up the summit rocks. Before we can follow they are down again. The wind higher up is impossibly dangerous. It's time to retreat.

A few months later I am at Fox Glacier for a reunion of mountain people organised as part of the centenary celebrations of the New Zealand Alpine Club. On the way I meet Cotter at Castle Rocks, near Arthurs Pass, where he is competing in a rock climbing meet. At Fox I meet his irascible father, Ed, a contemporary of Hillary and a member of the 1951 New Zealand quartet that made such an impact in the Himalayas.

It is a moving, unforgettable weekend but I have another reason for wangling to get there. Ball, who by now has summitted Everest and the highest peak on each of the world's seven continents, is paying his respects to the mountaineers of old too. And he has a few days to spare afterwards. We will fly over the Divide to Plateau Hut and climb Cook. When I go to bed around midnight the sky shines with starlight; at 4am it is raining. The Main Divide stays inaccessible for the next five days.

In November that year I am invited to walk the Milford Track. The tour is to end with an overnight at Mt Cook and a flight onto the Tasman Glacier. Ball is again between overseas guiding assignments so I persuade the Mt Cook Group to take us instead to Plateau Hut.

When we leave Milford the sun shines in a clear sky, but as we fly into Mt Cook hogs back (lenticular) clouds hover over the Divide. There will be no climbing for at least a week. It is surely time to give up, particularly after a couple of ski touring trips in the Mt Cook region are also thwarted by weather.

When Ball loses his life on Mt Dhaulagiri in 1993 I lose a dear friend. My Mt Cook incentive goes with him to his grave at the bottom of a Himalayan crevasse. But he does leave behind other persuasive guides. Cotter has been to the top of Everest with Ball and persuades me to try again – and my wife persuades a friend to join me.

We wait at Mt Cook for the wind to abate on the tops. After 10 years you get used to waiting, looking at weather maps, and asking locals for their assessment. Time is running out but Cotter reckons there is a weather window that might just give us enough time. So we fly in to the Grand Plateau late in the day, check our gear, eat and try to snatch a couple of hours' sleep before waking at 11pm.

The ritual of rope, crampons, head torch and ice axe is now familiar. Across the plateau and up into the Linda Glacier I feel good. Chris Smith, my companion, is guided by Nick Cradock, one of the country's foremost mountaineers and guides. Both he and Cotter climbed this peak when they were 15 years old.

Cotter says we are making really good time but after a couple of hours I feel sick and wooden-legged. I want to throw up but can't. It is not pleasant. If I rest the feeling tends to go but returns when I begin to climb again. Something is wrong. After 4 hours we are at the top of the glacier and about to traverse the ice shelf to the base of the summit rocks. It is a steep, diagonal traverse that guides usually take clients across on a short rope. It is no place for the clumsy. There is little chance of arresting a fall on the slope before it plunges over the shelf in a massive icefall.

We stop for a food break at a spot from where on my first attempt I had witnessed deadly blocks of ice cannon down the Gun Barrel only seconds after we had crossed the avalanche chute. I start to feel chilled. My stomach feels worse but it is time to move on. I think I'll be okay, but after just a few steps I say to Cotter, 'This is not a good idea. I think I should go down.' Cotter says he thinks I have made the right call. I have been stumbling for the last half hour. Altitude sickness is the likely cause. Chris elects to turn back too.

At first I am devastated, thoughts in a jumble of failure, embarrassment, annoyance, relief. By the time we get back to the hut I have sorted most of it out. I even feel proud of myself for having the experience to make a safe decision. I have learned more in this 10-year quest than I realised.

And I have been on this hill so many times, have climbed the route so often in my mind, that I don't feel robbed. The only problem is, what am I going to write about?

'You should write about yourself,' says Cradock, a man with not a shred of pretension and who doesn't suffer it in others either.

When I demur he says, 'You've been trying to climb this mountain for ten years. You've worked hard at it. You have done more on this mountain than a lot of people who have got to the top.'

When I get home my 10-year-old daughter puts it another way. 'Dad, if you put on end all the distance you have climbed you would have been up Mt Cook about three times.'

There is one other reason for this story. Cotter and Cradock suggest I have wasted a lot of climbing time by focusing on Cook. Forget it, they advise, at least until one day when you happen to be in the village and everything coincides. There are other mountains to climb.

Mountain guides are a persuasive lot.

Adventure, as with beauty, tends to be in the eye of the beholder. So when New Zealand's foremost adventurer Graeme Dingle talks about adventure it is likely that he has something personal in mind. Dingle is no elitist but he reckons, with some justification, that adventuring is getting a bit soft, that removing all risk also removes the spice of challenge. An adventure, says Dingle, has to have the thrill of an unknown outcome.

I tend to adopt the word in the manner of an old climbing mate, Mike Waterhouse, who prefixes all outdoor activities with his family and friends with the invitation to 'go and have an adventure'. The usage – and Waterhouse's activities – generally concurs with the dictates of *Herald* style, which demands the first definition in the Concise Oxford Dictionary: 'an unusual and exciting experience'.

The second definition – 'a daring enterprise; a hazardous activity' – is perhaps a little more Dingle-like. But if the lexicographers had ever been to Aoraki/Mt Cook, where Dingle and I are discussing the semantics of adventure, they might have just resolved the debate with the definition 'an experience at Mt Cook'.

For many kilometres all around us rise the soaring mountains and creeping glaciers that have been the scene of some of this country's most unusual, exciting, daring and hazardous adventures. Dingle himself has featured in several of the most noted and I know from bitter experience that the outcome of adventures here is often unknown.

In 1894 Malcolm Ross, a journalist accompanying those who a month later would be the first to scale Mt Cook, was forced to turn his back on days of rain and wind, disconsolately reflecting that 'for the man with a limited holiday, mountaineering is a game of chance with the weather, and that the weather generally holds at least three aces and a long suit.'

The sort of weather Ross experienced in 1894 has previously thwarted my own adventures on that peak. So it is novel that on this occasion, an alpine festival to celebrate the 100th anniversary of the first Mt Cook ascent, the problem should be with sunshine.

The mountains of the Southern Alps are thick with snow and at Mt Cook much of it has not had time to settle before being hit by the warmth of spring. The snow is deep, wet and quick to slide down any gully the sun settles on for too long. But if conditions or lack of time ever kept the high peaks out of bounds again, I have resolved that instead of being as disconsolate as Ross, I will follow the advice of Waterhouse and go and have an adventure.

The track from the Hermitage to Kea Point is a delightful 2- to 3-hour ramble up the Hooker valley, bounded on one side by Mt Wakefield and the apex of the Mt Cook Range, and on the other by the Sealy Range. Ahead is the Footstool, an arresting peak on which Dingle has left a bold route, but whose melting snow once defeated Waterhouse and me. And dominating all, at least until Mt Cook slips into view up the Hooker Glacier, are the stupendous hanging ice cliffs of Mt Sefton.

Kea Point gives a view over the lower Mueller Glacier and I know from a previous visit that in a month or so the track will sparkle in places with the brilliant white of giant mountain buttercups and mountain daisies. Later the brown tussock will bloom with the delicate mauves, pinks and blues of wild lupins and foxgloves. At present their leaves are just beginning to bud from dry stalks. To the right the track runs off towards the turbulent Hooker River and a glacier that leads almost all the way to the slopes of Mt Cook. But a valley trek can be left to a wet day, and I turn left towards the Sealy Range.

The track to Sealy Tarns is about the steepest and roughest trek close to Mount Cook village, climbing about 500m up the range from the Kea Point track. In the summer it takes a couple of comfortable hours from the Hermitage to get to the tarns nestling in an alpine meadow halfway to the crest of the range. It is not so comfortable when thick, wet snow settles in the hollows of the track and the skis strapped to my rucksack seem determined to catch in every piece of overhanging shrubbery.

It gets no easier as the track goes higher because the lower the shrubbery is to the ground, the higher the snow is under foot, knee and sometimes thigh. But there are eventually rewards for these labours. I stretch out on a large rock protruding from the snow and scrub and eat my lunch, boxed by the Hermitage, just as trekkers probably did 100 years ago.

The ice cliffs of Sefton now look remarkably close but even with field glasses I cannot make out tiny Sefton Bivvy on the slopes of the Footstool. It sleeps four people on its straw floor and is the oldest building in the park but now it

The golden sands of Abel Tasman National Park are an icon of the New Zealand outdoors.

Drinks break on the Queen Charlotte Walkway, where the views of the Marlborough Sounds go on forever.

The sun shines over the Liebig Range but not over the climbers on the summit rocks near the East Face of Mt Cook. (Gary Ball)

A 'There is a lot more to it' photo opportunity on the Grand Plateau.
Mt Cook looks inviting but the wind proves diabolical.

On the way to Mt Tapuae o Uenuku, in the Inland Kaikoura Range, via 66 crossings of the Hodder River.

is buried in snow. In the far distance of the Hooker Glacier is the classic southerly aspect of Mt Cook. The magnificence can actually be absorbed without effort, like bathing in a mineral pool, a sort of spiritual osmosis.

Only two things come to mar this process. The beat of an air force helicopter reverberates up the Hooker valley. If anyone wonders why some people don't like the idea of helicopters flight-seeing

adventure log

GETTING THERE: Fly into Mount Cook village or drive via Fairlie.

WALKING TIME: Sealy Tarns is a day walk from Mount Cook village but in summer you could overnight in Mueller Hut.

MAP: Aoraki/Mount Cook & Westland/Tai Poutini Parkmap 273-10.

FURTHER INFORMATION: Visit the DOC information centre at Mt Cook 0-3-435 1819 to get details of day walks from the village. Read OUTDOOR PURSUITS IN NEW ZEALAND by Graeme Dingle.

around mountains they should go sit on a sunny rock on the Sealy Range. The second disturbance is the regular slide of wet snow in the gullies around me. The avalanches start from tiny points, often where a rock protrudes. These slopes catch the full weight of the sun and experienced heads have advised me not to stay up here too long.

There is no way I can now reach Mueller Hut, which in summer provides a relatively close opportunity to experience the overnight atmosphere of a mountain hut and watch the splendour of an alpine sunset and sunrise. But the two sets of footprints ahead of me have now changed to skis so I do the same and, keeping clear of a gully full of avalanche debris, push on a little way further.

The snow-covered tarns give a false sense of comfort as I loosen my pack straps and slowly skin up the slope above them. The slides have been moving a lot slower than I can ski and this slope is not as steep as the gullies that border it.

When I pass the protection of a large rock bluff, the slope begins to steepen. It is time to turn around – but not here. Any sort of turn suddenly doesn't seem like a good idea. I gently move backwards in my tracks until I am protected by a rock before taking my skis off to remove the climbing skins. A small slide goes off beside me but only moves a couple of metres before stopping in a large crack in the snow. With skis back on and all straps undone, I gently ski back down my tracks to the alpine meadow flats that the tarns nestle in.

I am still strapping my skis to my rucksack when a snow slide begins by the rock I sheltered behind, moves over the deep crack in the snow and slowly fans out across the slope, covering the ungainly ski tracks I have made in the soft snow. It ends on the flat behind me, the debris about a metre high.

Bits are falling off Sefton, and elsewhere, with a distant roar and there are continuous slides in the gully beside me as I stride down the ridge and regain the Sealy Tarns track. In places the step plugs are thigh-deep. Sometimes the step risers, made from railway sleepers, hold back deep pools of melted snow. At times it is as though some hidden animal is lurking about because as the snow melts a branch of scrub will suddenly spring upwards as though it has been disturbed.

It is an enjoyable trek in the afternoon back to the Hermitage. When I meet up with Dingle in the evening I tell him about my hike and brief ski tour above Sealy Tarns.

'But was it an adventure?' he asks, grinning mischievously. I tell him I reckon it was – by any definition.

Mountains tend to inspire people and poets to superlatives, to expose raw emotion and spirituality. Among the more moving of homages is that from Freda du Faur, who in 1910 became the first woman to climb Aoraki/Mt Cook.

'From the moment my eyes rested on the snow-clad alps I worshipped their beauty and was filled with a passionate longing to touch those shining snows, to climb to their heights of silence and solitude, and to feel myself one with the mighty forces around me,' she wrote.

Du Faur, an Australian, was mesmerised by her first sight of the snow-capped peaks but she wanted to do more than merely observe their grandeur. 'My chief desire as I gazed at them was to reach the snow and bury my hands in its wonderful whiteness, and dig and dig till my snow-starved Australian soul was satisfied that all this wonder of white was real and would not vanish at the touch.'

Touch the mountains she did, including the first ever grand traverse of all three peaks of Aoraki – and not without a dig at the lounge-lizard tourists at the Hermitage for giving her a hard time for risking her 'reputation' by climbing alone with a guide. 'It is as natural to me to wish to climb as it is for the average New Zealander to be satisfied with peaceful contemplation from a distance,' she wrote.

But take heart if ever you are fortunate enough to pay some homage to du Faur's beloved alps, or any peak, because despite her remarkable efforts on the high peaks, she was quite happy too on 'picnics and scrambles' at much lower and less ambitious altitudes.

'Our favourite spot was a small tarn halfway up the Sebastopol, known as the Red Lake. Here we returned time and again, never tiring of the glorious view of Sefton and Mt Cook which it affords. The lake is almost covered with a coppery red water weed. I never saw such lovely lights – golden, purple, and bronze – as play upon this tarn, while on a still evening the reflections of the mountains add the finishing touch to its beauty.'

So a day when low cloud covers the tops of du Faur's snow-clad alps and mist hangs in the alpine valleys around the Hermitage seems a good one to check out a few Australian superlatives. Back in 1912 the redoubtable du Faur complained that since her last visit a 'paternal Government' had bridged the Black Birch Stream and gone were 'the exciting days when to cross it one must leap lightly from one slippery boulder to another, with the chance of an icy bath if the leap was unsuccessful.'

She wrote: 'The bridge gave me a regretful feeling that the mountains were fast becoming civilised, and I felt a pang such as no doubt assails the mountaineer in Switzerland when he sees a railway crawling up a beloved peak. Fortunately it will take a generation or two for New Zealand to arrive at such a state of barbarism. For a long while yet I hope the happy climber may still have his mountain all to himself, undefiled by railways, tourists and beer bottles.'

I am happy enough to use the bridge on this damp day but feel fortunate that it is likely no wider than when du Faur saw it and certainly there is no railway, nor tourist vans, to defile the track ahead. In fact, it looks as though I have the whole hillside to myself.

At the crest of the track there is a convenient wooden seat that even on this misty day invites a pause to check out the glorious views of Sefton and Mt Cook. At the tarns the water is still cold so the water weed, *Potamogeton cheesemanii*, seems quite ordinary – but not so the panorama behind the tarns.

Much of Mt Annette, the closest major peak here, is hidden by cloud but its outlier, Sebastopol, rears up free of mist to give the alpine lakes a dramatically realistic backdrop. For some reason the 1468m peak carries no 'Mt' prefix on my map. Perhaps 'Big Mick' Radove, the Sicilian runholder of Birch Hill Station who named the peak after the battle he had fought in while serving in the Royal Navy, considered it an unnecessary appendage.

Its snow-covered top, accentuated by broad scree slopes, is inviting – particularly as there is an obvious route up a slope above the tarns and someone I recognise as a ski-mountaineering guide is now walking up there with a young woman. Perhaps she had been reading du Faur and was not going to let a bit of rain on the tops – or the risk to reputation of being alone with a guide – keep her indoors.

The resolute pioneer had resisted the tearful pleading of one old lady not to 'spoil my life for so small a thing as climbing a mountain'. Instead at Red Tarns she lazed, 'dreaming in perfect contentment'. But she did enjoin anyone disposed to be energetic to climb to the top of Sebastopol.

There are some lengthy patches of soft snow to avoid but the track looks obvious and in summer is probably well worn. Near the rock bluffs that rear up to the summit the cloud starts to swirl down off Annette and the guide and his partner decide they have had enough Sunday strolling.

But I feel the need to 'bag a peak' and there is going to

adventure log

GETTING THERE: Fly into Mount Cook village or drive via Fairlie on State Highway 8.

CLIMBING TIME: Half a day – or an evening to watch the sunset.

MAP: Aoraki/Mount Cook & Westland/Tai Poutini Parkmap 273-10.

FURTHER INFORMATION: There is an extensive DOC information centre in the Mount Cook village where you can get brochures on short walks. DOC Aoraki Mount Cook 0-3-435 1819. Read THE CONQUEST OF MOUNT COOK by Freda du Faur and BETWEEN HEAVEN AND EARTH: THE LIFE OF A MOUNTAINEER, FREDA DU FAUR by Sally Irwin.

be none easier than this. It is easy climbing and before long the rocks give way to a snow-covered summit ridge. The previously unseen side is quite steeply corniced so I carefully check the snow with an alpenstock as I move to claim my summit.

Even on such a lowly peak as this, it is possible in the silence and solitude to become 'a little spiritual', as a famous guide, the late Harry Ayres, delightfully understated it.

As mountaineer Jill Tremain put it: 'What a privilege to know the profound stillness and peace of the land.'

Du Faur would surely concur.

in the footsteps of the rainbow god

It may be as well that Mt Tapuae o Uenuku is in the Inland Kaikoura Range, separated from the Pacific coast by the Clarence River and the Seaward Kaikoura Range. Among New Zealand's classic peaks, it shares with isolated Mt Tutoko in Fiordland the distinction of being the only mountain not to have been given a new name by early European explorers. How could they possibly match a name so romantic as the ancient and revered title, 'Footsteps of the Rainbow God'?

Not that 'Tappy' – as climbers dub it out of affection, not disrespect – is hidden away. It can be seen from more than 100km to the north, its snow-capped winter summit looming above Cook Strait, so tantalisingly close that the outdoors folk of Wellington look upon the 2885m peak as their own.

Tappy rises to 2500m in just 8km and were it just a bit closer to the eastern seaboard it would have been internationally famous when the sun dawned on the new millennium. Cartographers calculate that there is just half a second between the sun striking the Rainbow God's Footsteps and the 1752m high summit of Mt Hikurangi, near the North Island's East Cape.

The Kaikouras are young mountains, being pushed into the sky by colliding plates on the earth's crust at more than 7mm a year – but without being subject to the same erosion as the rain-swept Southern Alps, where lie the only mountains higher than Mt Tapuae o Uenuku. For the present, I consider Tappy to be quite high enough as I plod up the Hodder River with Andy Cole, an air force avionics technician and member of Woodbourne's SAR team, who has kindly agreed to take me to this classic summit.

The first day will be the toughest, he promises, and so it proves. The approach is up the boulder-strewn Hodder River and requires a reputed 66 river crossings. We can measure our progress up to the Hodder huts by how much in leaf are clusters of deciduous mountain ribbonwood, one of only two New Zealand deciduous natives. As we climb higher the leaf buds have barely emerged.

After more than 7 hours of step-ups, I am as knackered as Cole predicted and the huts, some 60m of steep climbing above the river-bed, might as well be a mile away. So when Cole, a Mountain Safety Council instructor, suggests I drop my pack I have no pride left to swallow and gladly accept. In the event, my pack is brought up to the hut by one of a group

adventure log

GETTING THERE: South of Blenheim turn west on the Awatere Valley Road. Follow a winding unsealed road for about 50km.

CLIMBING TIME: A day to walk in, a day to climb and a day to walk out.

MAP: LINZ S35.

FURTHER INFORMATION: Read GREAT PEAKS OF NEW ZEALAND by Hugh Logan and GREAT TRAMPS FOR NEW ZEALANDERS by Mark Pickering and Rodney Smith.

from the Nelson Tramping Club, who on legs longer and younger than mine have sauntered up the Hodder in about 2 hours less than us.

The original Hodder Hut of six bunks was built by the Tararua Tramping Club in 1975 and later passed on to the Marlborough Tramping Club. In 1988 the Marlborough trampers built a 14-bunk hut alongside the original. It is anniversary weekend in Marlborough and with our arrival all the bunks are full.

Our Nelson hut mates leave for the summit in the early hours of the morning in search of still frozen snow that will make cramponing easier. Cole wants reasonable light to cross a scree slope near the huts. It proves a wise decision for as we prepare to leave we can see the torchlights of the young enthusiasts way off the trail, needlessly climbing a substantial hillock.

In daylight the trail is easily followed and I imagine that by the end of summer it will be well trod. We are following the classic route up Staircase Creek into basins beneath the saddle that separates Tappy from its slightly smaller neighbour, Mt Alarm. The route was climbed in 1864 by Nehemiah McRaie, who left a bottle containing a £5 note on the summit.

Fingers of snow reach down towards our path and they are still firm, so we attach our crampons and move more directly up a couloir toward the summit's south-west ridge. Fortunately the snow stays firm as we crampon on to the ridge. The summit appears at about the same time as the Nelson party meets us on their descent, having climbed a different basin and snow slope.

The final part of the ridge is a little exposed, dropping away to the Clarence River, but the views are stunning. The Richmond Range and Spenser Mountains lie in the distance in the direction we have come, and to the north-east is

Wellington and the North Island. There is a steel pipe at the summit but McRaie's money has gone. We take a panoramic lunch before retracing our footsteps and sinking to our knees down slopes that have now felt the sun for some time.

I arrive back at the huts to the compliments of the young Nelsonians and, though tired, I feel pretty good about climbing the second-highest peak outside the Cook region, even if not quite in the manner of Sir Edmund Hillary, who once cycled from the Woodbourne Air Base and completed the climb in the space of a weekend's leave.

Hugh Logan, chief executive of the Department of Conservation, says in his book *Great Peaks* that 'to know Tapuae o Uenuku is to know one of New Zealand's great mountains'.

And I can say I know it.

escape by kayak

It is likely enough to make a wonky-kneed tramper spit. Here we are, camped on a deserted beach in Tennyson Inlet in the Marlborough Sounds, with all our gear and food for a week, and Glen is dicing fresh cauliflower and courgettes into his billy.

'The word kayak has got nothing to do with Eskimos,' he explains between sips of a refreshing cold beer.

'It is actually derived from kai, meaning food, and yak, meaning to carry great loads.'

A few metres further down the beach smoke spirals lazily from a driftwood fire on which Laurie, Liz, Richard and Nick cook huge, succulent mussels, plucked from the shoreline in ankle-deep water.

Our tents are nestled in the flax and scrub of Tawa Bay, our bright sea kayaks pulled up above the high-tide mark. A persistent weka keeps getting in to the cockpit of Andy's canoe. He yells at it in his native German, but the bird doesn't seem to understand.

Who knows what the rich people are doing? Who cares?

With 1500km of coastal inlets, the drowned valleys of the Marlborough Sounds Maritime Park are ideal for sea-kayak touring. It is a spectacularly odd region. The steep ridges of land that rise abruptly from the sounds have been conveyed by the alpine fault 450km north of their cousin rocks in Otago. And they continue to move towards Wellington at an average of 6.6mm a year.

In the clash of the Earth's crustal plates that has caused the movement, the sounds, which are on the Pacific plate that is being overridden, are getting slowly pushed beneath the sea. That makes the sounds the only large land area in the country that is sinking and not rising. And for the sea-kayak tourist, the geology of the sounds means it can be difficult to find enough flat space on the shoreline on which to pitch a party's tents.

Fortunately DOC has told us of several sites that had no facilities but are suitable for camping. As well, there are DOC camp-sites, particularly in Kenepuru and Queen Charlotte Sounds, with toilet and water facilities. These usually have water access only and cost $2 a night, the money placed in an envelope in an honesty box.

A gentle $1^1/_2$-hour paddle down the deeply wooded Tennyson Inlet brings us to Tawa Bay, our first experience of Marlborough Sounds mussels and the antics of the mischievous weka. Nothing is sacred to the weka; leave any small item lying around and they will scurry off into the undergrowth with it.

Our kayaking plans have a bit of the weka about them too. The declared strategy is that if the weather is suitable all or some of us will head for the outer sounds and rugged D'Urville Island, where Maori quarried argillite to make adzes and early European settlers mined copper.

But we are advised that paddling around the island and through the pass that sent D'Urville's *Astrolabe* turning end-for-end several times, is fraught with severe rips, strong winds, and hazardous tidal flows. What to do? There is much deliberating around the campfire, but in the end an uncertain weather forecast decides it for us and a compromise plan is hatched. We will paddle across the inlet to Hallam Cove, park our kayaks in Burnside Bay and then walk down the French Pass road for the sort of view that D'Urville climbed a hill to see before sailing his corvette through the pass.

Someone reckoned that it is just a 5km walk along this ridge traverse high above Pelorus Sound and Tasman Bay; about 15km of tortuously winding road later we see the white water and pressure waves of the pass. By the time the return journey is completed the wonder of the bird's-eye views of Admiralty Bay, Tasman Bay, D'Urville Island and outer Pelorus Sound has long lost its impact.

We are late into our campsite at Waiona Bay that night and the rain soon follows. Wet nights and dry days are the pattern for the rest of our trip, which means a daily ritual of wet packing – and wonderful paddling.

From Pelorus Sound we move into the beautifully wooded Kenepuru Sound and trundle our kayaks across the Portage to Queen Charlotte. In places shag chicks eye us from a couple of metres above our kayaks. It would be difficult to find a more pleasant spot than Ratimera Bay, the pick of our campsites.

On our last day we paddle down Queen Charlotte Sound to Picton, past williwaws coming down the many valleys and occasionally nasty little seas thrown up off the headlands by wind and tide.

It is an exhilarating conclusion to a particularly special journey.

a royal foot road

From Abbey to West Hoe, the Southern Alps are filled with mountain passes. So a perversely logical question keeps bothering me as I become another of the 11,000 pairs of feet that make the annual tramp across Mackinnon Pass. Without this track and our boots on it, would it be any better known than Kehua Pass? And would it deserve to be?

By day three it has become an all-consuming conundrum. A track is by dictionary definition a rough path 'beaten by use'. So is the Milford Track 'the finest walk in the world' just because for more than 100 years people have been beating a path over its 55km? If there were no people using it, would it be just an old route across the spine of New Zealand and just another pass through the Alps?

There are at least 245 people walking along the trail with me every day. But I have hardly seen sight or sign of them. In front and behind me the track appears deserted, fallen leaves are barely disturbed and a thin layer of moss still covers rocks that lie like flagstones in the path.

But this is the Milford Track, the route that in 1903 the fledgling Department of Tourist and Health Resorts billed as a 'tourist foot road' to Milford. The State and now private enterprise have been guiding tourists along it ever since – 42 people a day, six days a week, between November and April, staying in fully serviced lodges. And since 1966 up to 40 independent trampers have set out each day, too. Yet it looks like Scottish surveyor Quinton Mackinnon blazed his trail up the Clinton valley from the head of Lake Te Anau only yesterday.

Mackinnon had an acute entrepreneurial instinct and when on 17 October 1888 he struggled to the top of the alpine pass that bears his name he wasn't thinking of colonists but the painters' retreat another Scot, Donald Sutherland, had set up in Milford Sound. Within months the canny Mackinnon was guiding tourists along his track. Twenty-four years later a British travel writer and poet, Blanche Baughan, labelled his walk the finest in the world and people have been coming in droves ever since.

Today another bunch sits to get its pre-walk briefing. We are heading into a park with World Heritage listing and the air is thick with foreign accents. But we are advised that by the end of the walk we will be a close-knit, supportive little community.

The historic launch *Tawera*, launched on Lake Te Anau in 1899, takes us and the day's group of independent walkers to the head of the lake and the start of the track. It's a bit of an anticlimax after all the preparations because Glade House is just a casual stroll from the jetty. The freedom walkers move off to their hut a couple of hours up the track and remain elusively in the distance for the next three days.

After dinner at Glade House, Terry and Hinga Fell, who run the hut, do a job they should try at the United Nations. Fell spent 30 years in the army before joining the Milford Track staff. His idea of war games now is to have a robust German trying to blow a ping-pong ball across a table against the power of a shapely American cheerleader.

Having won that skirmish the Americans take on the Aussies at passing oranges under their chins. Our Tasman cousins are a bit embarrassed because they don't know the words to their national anthem; a couple of urban sophisticates are embarrassed at the whole thing because they are urbane sophisticates.

But when Hinga Fell leads the Kiwi contingent in Pokarekare Ana you can tell from the rapturous faces that the battle is won already – with the track still in front of us waiting to be 'beaten by use'. It seems so corny but it works.

'It ought to, we've been doing it for a hundred years,' says Terry Fell.

When we set off next morning following the west branch of the Clinton River to the Pompolona Huts, we are a cohesive unit that Warrant Officer Fell would have been proud of. Yet, and here's where the conundrum first begins gnawing, we are soon walking through the dappled beech forest and peering into the gin-clear Clinton alone – undisturbed in our own little world of wonder and awe.

There are several reasons for this. The Milford Track is point-to-point one way, so no one ever comes walking towards you. Everyone, freedom walkers included, must stay in designated huts so all are moving along at the same pace. But probably the most significant reason is the number of stops people make to take photographs of the ever-changing views. It leaves us alone in our reverie.

I shoot more rolls of film than I have ever done on a three-week holiday, but nowhere near as much as Klaus and Krista Lewandowski of Elmshorn,

Germany. They are keen amateur photographers and travel with two cameras each and a tripod that they set up to capture subtle changes in light and the contrast of the snowy tops of Clinton Canyon.

I am busy chasing trout in crystal pools, although I soon give away any thoughts of catching one and am content to just admire the precocious beauty. Russell Dun, a 68-year-old retired Tauranga vet who carries a fishing rod, too, reckons the trout are looking up and laughing at us. Jerry Bronicel from Salt Lake City doesn't care; he is grinning as much as the trout he flicks a line at.

I keep running into Jerry because when he is not fishing he is pointing his video camera and smiling. It's just as well, too, because he keeps dropping bits and pieces of his gear on the track. It's easy to leave something behind; the views all around are literally stunning. We can look up without fear, too, because for some reason we are spared even a drop of Milford's renowned 6259mm annual fall of rain.

That is actually a pity because if there is just one shower waterfalls by the dozen would cascade down from the canyon tops to send Klaus and Krista into raptures. As it is there is no shortage of falls and the mighty Sutherland Falls give some of our raincoats the ultimate test.

Our guide is in his seventh season. At night when we re-form our cohesive unit, he puts on an after-dinner slide show. It reminds us of that which now binds us together and sends us to sleep with pleasant dreams of what the morrow will bring. Yet even dreams cannot capture the ethereal beauty and rich fragrance of the moss-covered forests of the tree fuchsia kotukutuku.

There are several signs of avalanche in the canyon. Now, as we zig-zag up and over Mackinnon Pass through a rich display of Mt Cook lilies, we can see avalanche debris off the Jervois Glacier. It buries the track under 4.5m of ice and we must descend a steeper, uneven emergency track.

At Quintin our hosts, Marlene and Brian Hancock, greet us with cold beers and a 'welcome to our house'.

The track has had two days to work its magic. Everyone is on a high. 'Walking through this country is a humbling experience,' says Marlene Hancock. 'People who want to spend $1000 on a walk somewhere are a special kind of people. We have more overseas people than New Zealanders, which is really sad.'

It's a long but easy-walking stroll down the Arthur valley to Sandfly Point, which in the chill of early summer poses no threat to human flesh. I briefly keep pace with the tall and athletic Brian and Annie Mooney, young San Francisco lawyers on their honeymoon. Like most of the overseas visitors in our group, the track is almost the only thing they have planned for their stay in New Zealand. The Milford Track is famous, you know.

At Lake Ada, Jerry Bronicel and two young German merchant bankers go trout fishing with a guide and rejoin us at the jetty near Sandfly Point triumphant. That night at Milford we celebrate our walk, our new friends and the certificate and group photograph we proudly claim – with an entrée of Jerry's brown trout.

The former United States Navy pilot is as proud as we are pleased for him. The conundrum is resolved. The Milford Track may be the finest in the world, but walking it is even better.

adventure log

GETTING THERE: All Milford Track trips, guided and independent, leave from Te Anau.

WALKING TIME: 4 days, whether you are fast or slow.

MAP: Milford Trackmap 335-01.

FURTHER INFORMATION: The trackmap has all the track information you will need. See also NEW ZEALAND WILDERNESS WALKS by Colin Moore and NEW ZEALAND'S GREAT WALKS Pearl Hewson. Te Anau Great Walks bookings 0-3-249 8514; guided walks 0-3-441 1138.